COOKSHELF

Pasta

p

This is a Parragon Publishing Book
This edition published in 2004

Parragon Publishing
Queen Street House
4 Queen Street
Bath BA1 1HE, UK

ISBN: 0-75255-522-7

Printed in China

Note
Cup measurements in this book are for American cups. Tablespoons are
assumed to be 15 ml. Unless otherwise stated, milk is assumed to be full fat,
eggs are medium and pepper is freshly ground black pepper.

Contents

Introduction

Pasta has existed since the days of the Roman Empire and remains one of the most versatile cooking ingredients: no storecupboard should be without it. It can be combined with meat, fish, vegetables, fruit or even a simple herb sauce to create a mouthwatering and nutritious meal within minutes.

Most pasta is made from durum wheat flour and contains protein and carbohydrates. It is a good source of slow-release energy and has the additional advantage of being value for money.

There are many different types of pasta, some of which are listed on the opposite page. Many are available both dried and fresh. Unless you have access to a good, Italian delicatessen, it is probably not worth buying fresh unfilled pasta, but even supermarkets sell high-quality tortellini, capelletti, ravioli, and agnolotti.

Best of all, is to make fresh pasta at home. It takes a little time, but is quite easy and well worth the effort. You can mix the dough by hand or prepare it in a food processor.

Pasta may be colored and flavored with extra ingredients that are usually added with the beaten egg:

Black: add 1 tsp squid or cuttlefish ink.
Green: add 4 ounces well-drained, cooked spinach when kneading.
Purple: thoroughly process 1 large, cooked beet in a food processor, and add with an extra ½ cup flour.
Red: add 2 tbsp tomato paste.

To cook pasta, bring a large pan of lightly salted water to a boil. Add the pasta and 1 tbsp olive oil, but do not cover or the water will boil over. Quickly bring the water back to a rolling boil and avoid overcooking. When the pasta is tender, but still firm to the bite, drain and toss with butter, olive oil, or your prepared sauce. The cooking times given here are guidelines only:

Fresh unfilled pasta: *2–3 minutes*
Fresh filled pasta: *8–10 minutes*
Dried unfilled pasta: *10–12 minutes*
Dried filled pasta: *15–20 minutes*

BASIC PASTA DOUGH

If you wish to make your own pasta for the dishes in this book, follow this simple recipe.

Serves 4

INGREDIENTS

4 cups durum wheat flour
4 eggs, lightly beaten
1 tbsp olive oil
salt

1 Lightly flour a counter. Sift the flour with a pinch of salt into a mound. Make a well in the center and add the eggs and olive oil.

2 Using a fork or your fingertips, gradually work the mixture until the ingredients are combined. Knead vigorously for 10–15 minutes.

3 Set the dough aside to rest for 25 minutes, before rolling it out as thinly and evenly as possible.

TYPES OF PASTA

There are as many as 200 different pasta shapes and about three times as many names for them. New shapes are being designed—and named—all the time and the same shape may be called a different name in different regions of Italy.

anelli, anellini: *small rings for soup*

bucatini: *long, medium-thick tubes*

cannelloni: *large, thick, round pasta tubes*

capelli d'angelo: *thin strands of 'angel hair'*

conchiglie: *ridged shells*

conchigliette: *little shells*

cresti di gallo: *curved-shaped*

ditali, ditalini: *short tubes*

eliche: *loose spirals*

farfalle: *bows*

fettuccine: *medium ribbons*

fusilli: *spirals*

gemelli: *two pieces wrapped together as 'twins'*

lasagne: *flat, rectangular sheets*

linguini: *long, flat ribbons*

lumache: *snail-shaped shells*

lumaconi: *big shells*

macaroni: *long- or short-cut tubes*

orecchiette: *ear-shaped*

penne: *quill-shaped*

rigatoni: *thick, ridged tubes*

spaghetti: *fine or medium rods*

tagliarini: *thin ribbons*

tagliatelle: *broad ribbons*

vermicelli: *fine pasta, usually folded into skeins*

Cannelloni

Fusilli

Conchigliette

Conchiglie

Orecchiette tricolori

Rigatoni

Lumaconi

Fettuccine

Spaghetti

Soups & Light Meals

Pasta is so versatile: it can be used to make soups more substantial, as a delicious and unusual starter, or as a quick and easy lunch or light supper. The recipes in this chapter range from traditional Italian dishes, such as Minestrone soup and Spaghetti alla Carbonara, to intriguing new ways with pasta, such as Pancetta & Pecorino Cakes with Farfalle and Pasta Omelet.

Soup recipes include filling winter dishes that, if served with some crusty bread, make a meal in themselves. Try Navy Bean & Pasta Soup, for example. Others, like Cream of Lemon & Chicken Soup, are subtle and delicate. Recipes for snacks and light meals offer something for every taste—vegetable, cheese, meat, and fish sauces combined with every pasta shape from linguine to lumache. Try Smoked Ham Linguine if you are in a hurry, or Creamed Veal Kidneys with Penne if you want something a little different.

Minestrone

Serves 8–10

INGREDIENTS

3 garlic cloves
3 large onions
2 celery sticks
2 large carrots
2 large potatoes
$3^1/2$ ounces green beans
$3^1/2$ ounces zucchini
4 tbsp butter
$^1/2$ cup olive oil

2 ounces fatty bacon, finely
　diced
$6^7/8$ cups vegetable or
　chicken stock
1 bunch fresh basil, finely
　chopped
$3^1/2$ ounces chopped
　tomatoes
2 tbsp tomato paste

$3^1/2$ ounces Parmesan cheese
　rind
3 ounces dried spaghetti,
　broken up
salt and pepper
freshly grated Parmesan
　cheese, to serve

1 Finely chop the garlic, onions, celery, carrots, potatoes, beans, and zucchini using a sharp knife.

2 Heat the butter and oil together in a large saucepan, add the bacon and cook for 2 minutes. Add the garlic and onion and fry for 2 minutes, then stir in the celery, carrots, and potatoes and fry for 2 minutes longer, stirring the vegetables occasionally.

3 Add the beans to the saucepan and fry for 2 minutes. Stir in the zucchini and cook for 2 minutes longer. Cover and cook all the vegetables, stirring frequently, for about 15 minutes.

4 Add the stock, basil, tomatoes, tomato paste, and cheese rind and season to taste. Bring to a boil, lower the heat and simmer for 1 hour. Remove and discard the cheese rind.

5 Add the spaghetti pieces to the pan and cook for 20 minutes. Serve sprinkled with freshly grated Parmesan cheese.

Italian Cream of Tomato Soup

Serves 4

INGREDIENTS

4 tbsp unsalted butter
1 large onion, chopped
2¹/2 cups vegetable stock
2 pounds Italian plum
    tomatoes, skinned and
    roughly chopped

pinch of baking soda
2 cups dried fusilli
1 tbsp superfine sugar
⁵/8 cup heavy cream
salt and pepper

fresh basil leaves, to garnish
deep-fried croutons, to serve

1 Melt the butter in a large saucepan, add the onion and sauté for 3 minutes. Add 1¼ cups of the vegetable stock to the saucepan, with the chopped tomatoes and baking soda. Bring the soup to a boil and simmer for 20 minutes.

2 Remove the pan from the heat and set aside to cool slightly. Purée the soup in a blender or food processor and pour through a fine strainer back into the saucepan.

3 Add the remaining vegetable stock and the fusilli to the pan, and season to taste.

4 Add the sugar to the pan, bring to a boil, then lower the heat and simmer for about 15 minutes.

5 Pour the soup into a warm tureen, swirl the heavy cream around the surface of the soup and garnish with fresh basil leaves. Serve immediately with croutons.

VARIATION

To make orange and tomato soup, simply use half the quantity of vegetable stock, topped off with the same amount of fresh orange juice and garnish the soup with orange rind. Or to make tomato and carrot soup, add half the quantity again of vegetable stock with the same amount of carrot juice and 1¼ cups grated carrot to the recipe, cooking the carrot with the onion.

Potato & Parsley Soup with Pesto

Serves 4

INGREDIENTS

3 slices bacon
1 pound mealy potatoes
1 pound onions
2 tbsp butter
2^1/$_2$ cups chicken stock
2^1/$_2$ cups milk
^{3}/$_4$ cup dried conchigliette
^{5}/$_8$ cup heavy cream
chopped fresh parsley
salt and black pepper

freshly grated Parmesan
   cheese and garlic bread, to
   serve

PESTO SAUCE:
1 cup finely chopped fresh
   parsley
2 garlic cloves, crushed
^{2}/$_3$ cup pine nuts, crushed

2 tbsp chopped fresh basil
   leaves
^{2}/$_3$ cup freshly grated
   Parmesan cheese
white pepper
^{5}/$_8$ cup olive oil

1 To make the pesto sauce, work all of the ingredients in a blender or food processor for 2 minutes, or blend together by hand (see Cook's Tip).

2 Finely chop the bacon, potatoes, and onions. Fry the bacon in a large pan for 4 minutes. Add the butter, potatoes, and onions and cook for 12 minutes, stirring constantly.

3 Add the stock and milk to the pan, bring to a boil, and simmer for 10 minutes. Add the conchigliette and simmer for 12-14 minutes.

4 Blend in the cream and simmer for 5 minutes. Add the parsley and 2 tbsp pesto sauce. Transfer the soup to serving bowls and serve with Parmesan cheese and fresh garlic bread.

COOK'S TIP

If you are making pesto by hand, it is best to use a mortar and pestle. Thoroughly grind together the parsley, garlic, pine nuts, and basil to make a paste, then mix in the cheese and pepper. Finally, gradually beat in the oil.

Ravioli alla Parmigiana

Serves 4

INGREDIENTS

10 ounces Basic Pasta Dough
(see page 4)
5 cups veal stock
freshly grated Parmesan
cheese, to serve

FILLING:
1 cup freshly grated Parmesan
cheese
1²/₃ cup fine white
breadcrumbs
2 eggs

¹/₂ cup espagnole sauce (see
Cook's Tip)
1 small onion, finely chopped
1 tsp freshly grated nutmeg

1 Make the basic pasta
dough (see page 4).
Carefully roll out 2 sheets
of the pasta dough and
cover with a damp dish
cloth while you prepare the
filling for the ravioli.

2 To make the filling,
mix together the
freshly grated Parmesan
cheese, fine white
breadcrumbs, eggs,
espagnole sauce (see
Cook's Tip), finely
chopped onion, and the
freshly grated nutmeg in a
large mixing bowl.

3 Place spoonfuls of the
filling at regular
intervals on 1 sheet of pasta
dough. Cover with the
second sheet of pasta
dough, then cut into
squares and seal the edges.

4 Bring the veal stock to
a boil in a large
saucepan. Add the ravioli to
the pan and cook for about
15 minutes.

5 Transfer the soup and
ravioli to warm serving
bowls and serve at once,
sprinkled with Parmesan.

COOK'S TIP

*For espagnole sauce, melt 2 tbsp
butter and stir in ¹/₄ cup all-
purpose flour. Cook over a low
heat, stirring, until lightly
colored. Add 1 tsp tomato paste,
then stir in 1¹/₄ cups hot veal
stock, 1 tbsp Madeira, and
1¹/₂ tsp white wine vinegar.
Dice 1 ounce each bacon,
carrot, and onion and ¹/₂ ounce
each celery, leek, and fennel.
Cook with a thyme sprig and a
bay leaf in oil until soft. Drain,
add to the sauce, and simmer
for 4 hours. Strain before using.*

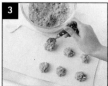

Pea & Egg Noodle Soup with Parmesan Cheese Croutons

Serves 4

INGREDIENTS

3 slices bacon, diced
1 large onion, chopped
1 tbsp butter
2 1/2 cups dried peas, soaked in cold water for 2 hours and drained

10 cups chicken stock
8 ounces dried egg noodles
5/8 cup heavy cream
salt and pepper

chopped fresh parsley, to garnish
Parmesan cheese croutons (see Cook's Tip), to serve

1 Put the bacon, onion, and butter into a large saucepan and cook over a low heat for 6 minutes.

2 Add the peas and the chicken stock to the pan and bring to a boil. Season lightly with salt and pepper, cover, and simmer for 1½ hours.

3 Add the noodles to the pan and simmer for an additional 15 minutes.

4 Pour in the cream and blend thoroughly. Transfer to a warm tureen, garnish with parsley, and top with Parmesan cheese croutons (see Cook's Tip). Serve immediately.

VARIATION

Use other legumes, such as dried navy beans, borlotti, or pinto beans, instead of the peas.

COOK'S TIP

To make Parmesan cheese croutons, cut a baguette into slices. Coat each slice lightly with olive oil and sprinkle with Parmesan cheese. Broil for about 30 seconds.

Navy Bean & Pasta Soup

Serves 4

INGREDIENTS

1¹/₃ cups navy beans, soaked
    for 3 hours in cold water
    and drained
4 tbsp olive oil
2 large onions, sliced
3 garlic cloves, chopped
14 ounce can chopped
    tomatoes
1 tsp dried oregano

1 tsp tomato paste
3¹/₂ cups water
³/₄ cup dried fusilli
    or conchigliette
4 ounces sun-dried tomatoes,
    drained and thinly sliced
1 tbsp chopped fresh cilantro
    or flat leaf parsley
salt and pepper

2 tbsp Parmesan cheese
    shavings, to serve

1 Put the navy beans in a large pan. Cover with cold water and bring to a boil. Boil vigorously for 15 minutes. Drain and keep warm.

2 Heat the oil in a pan over a medium heat and sauté the onions for 2–3 minutes. Stir in the garlic and cook for 1 minute. Stir in the tomatoes, oregano, and tomato paste.

3 Add the water and the reserved beans to the pan. Bring to a boil, cover, then simmer for about 45 minutes, or until the beans are almost tender.

4 Add the pasta to the pan and season to taste. Stir in the sun-dried tomatoes, bring back to a boil, partly cover, and simmer for 10 minutes, or until the pasta is tender, but still firm to the bite.

5 Stir the cilantro or parsley into the soup. Ladle the soup into a warm tureen, sprinkle with the Parmesan and serve.

COOK'S TIP

If desired, place the beans in a pan of cold water and bring to a boil. Remove from the heat and leave the beans to cook in the water. Drain and rinse before using.

Garbanzo Bean & Chicken Soup

Serves 4

INGREDIENTS

2 tbsp butter
3 scallions, chopped
2 garlic cloves, crushed
1 fresh marjoram sprig,
   finely chopped
12 ounces boned chicken
   breasts, diced

5 cups chicken stock
12 ounce can garbanzo
   beans, drained
1 bouquet garni
1 red bell pepper, diced
1 green bell pepper, diced

1 cup small dried pasta
   shapes, such as elbow
   macaroni
salt and white pepper
croutons, to serve

1 Melt the butter in a large saucepan. Add the scallions, garlic, sprig of fresh marjoram, and the diced chicken to the saucepan and cook, stirring frequently, over a medium heat for 5 minutes.

2 Add the chicken stock, garbanzo beans, and bouquet garni to the saucepan and then season to taste with salt and white pepper.

3 Bring the soup to a boil, lower the heat, and then simmer gently for about 2 hours.

4 Add the diced bell peppers and pasta to the pan, then simmer for 20 minutes longer.

5 Transfer the soup to a warm tureen. To serve, ladle the soup into individual serving bowls and serve immediately, garnished with the croutons.

COOK'S TIP

If preferred, use dried garbanzo beans. Cover with cold water and set aside to soak for 5–8 hours. Drain and add the beans to the soup, according to the recipe, and allow an additional 30 minutes–1 hour cooking time.

Cream of Lemon & Chicken Soup with Spaghetti

Serves 4

INGREDIENTS

4 tbsp butter
8 shallots, thinly sliced
2 carrots, thinly sliced
2 celery stalks, thinly sliced
8 ounces boned chicken
   breasts, finely chopped
3 lemons

5 cups chicken stock
8 ounces dried spaghetti,
   broken into small pieces
5/8 cup heavy cream
salt and white pepper

TO GARNISH:
fresh parsley sprig
3 lemon slices, halved

1 Melt the butter in a large saucepan. Add the shallots, carrots, celery, and chicken and cook over a low heat, stirring occasionally, for 8 minutes.

2 Thinly pare the lemons and blanch the lemon rind in boiling water for 3 minutes. Squeeze the juice from the lemons.

3 Add the lemon rind and juice to the pan, together with the chicken stock. Slowly bring to a boil and simmer for 40 minutes.

4 Add the spaghetti to the pan and cook for 15 minutes. Season to taste with salt and white pepper and add the cream. Heat through, but do not allow the soup to boil or it will curdle.

5 Pour the soup into a tureen or individual bowls, garnish with the parsley and half slices of lemon, and serve immediately.

COOK'S TIP

You can prepare this soup up to the end of step 3 in advance, so that all you need do before serving is heat it through before adding the pasta and the finishing touches.

Chicken & Corn Soup

Serves 4

| INGREDIENTS |

1 pound boned chicken
breasts, cut into strips
5 cups chicken stock

$^5/_8$ cup heavy cream
$^3/_4$ cup dried vermicelli
1 tbsp cornstarch
3 tbsp milk

6 ounces corn kernels
salt and pepper

1 Put the chicken, stock, and cream into a large saucepan and slowly bring to a boil. Reduce the heat slightly and simmer for about 20 minutes. Season to taste.

2 Meanwhile, cook the vermicelli in lightly salted boiling water for 10-12 minutes, until just tender. Drain the pasta and keep warm.

3 In a small bowl, mix together the cornstarch and milk to make a smooth paste. Stir the cornstarch paste into the soup until thickened.

4 Add the corn and vermicelli to the saucepan and heat through.

5 Transfer the soup to a warm tureen or individual soup bowls and serve immediately.

COOK'S TIP

If you are short of time, buy ready-cooked chicken, remove any skin, and cut it into slices.

VARIATION

For crab and corn soup, substitute 1 pound cooked crabmeat for the chicken breasts. Flake the crabmeat thoroughly before adding it to the saucepan and reduce the cooking time by 10 minutes. For a Chinese-style soup, substitute egg noodles for the vermicelli and use canned, creamed corn.

Veal & Ham Soup with Sherry

Serves 4

INGREDIENTS

4 tbsp butter	$^1/_2$ cup all-purpose flour	$^5/_8$ cup cream sherry
1 onion, diced	$4^3/_8$ cups beef stock	$^3/_4$ cup dried vermicelli
1 carrot, diced	1 bay leaf	garlic croutons, to serve
1 celery stalk, diced	8 black peppercorns	
1 pound very thinly sliced veal	pinch of salt	
1 pound thinly sliced ham	3 tbsp red currant jelly	

1 Melt the butter in a large saucepan. Cook the onions, carrot, celery, veal, and ham over a low heat for about 6 minutes.

2 Sprinkle in the flour and cook, stirring constantly, for a further 2 minutes. Gradually stir in the stock, then add the bay leaf, peppercorns, and salt. Bring to a boil and simmer for 1 hour.

3 Remove the pan from the heat and add the red currant jelly and cream sherry. Set aside for about 4 hours.

4 Remove and discard the bay leaf. Reheat the soup over a very low heat until warmed through.

5 Meanwhile, cook the vermicelli in a pan of lightly salted boiling water for 10-12 minutes. Stir the vermicelli into the soup and transfer to warm soup bowls. Serve with garlic croutons (see Cook's Tip).

COOK'S TIP

To make garlic croutons, remove the crusts from 3 slices of day-old white bread. Cut the bread into $^1/_4$ inch cubes. Heat 3 tbsp olive oil and stir-fry 1–2 finely chopped garlic cloves for 1–2 minutes. Remove the garlic and add the bread. Cook, tossing the pan and stirring frequently, until golden brown. Remove from the pan with a slotted spoon and drain on paper towels.

Tuscan Veal Broth

Serves 4

INGREDIENTS

$^1/_3$ cup dried peas, soaked for
   2 hours and drained
2 pounds boned neck of
   veal, diced
5 cups beef or brown stock
   (see Cook's Tip)
$2^1/_2$ cups water

$^1/_3$ cup barley, washed
1 large carrot, diced
1 small turnip (about
   6 ounces), diced
1 large leek, thinly sliced
1 red onion, finely chopped

$3^1/_2$ ounces chopped
   tomatoes
1 fresh basil sprig
$^3/_4$ cup dried vermicelli
salt and white pepper

1   Put the peas, veal, stock, and water into a large pan and bring to a boil over a low heat. Skim off any film that rises to the surface of the liquid.

2   When all of the film has been removed, add the barley and a pinch of salt to the mixture. Simmer gently over a low heat for 25 minutes.

3   Add the carrot, turnip, leek, onion, tomatoes, and basil to the pan, and season to taste. Simmer for about 2 hours, skimming the surface with a slotted spoon, from time to time. Remove the pan from the heat and set aside for 2 hours.

4   Set the pan over a medium heat and bring to a boil. Add the vermicelli and cook for 12 minutes. Season with salt and pepper to taste and remove and discard the basil. Ladle the soup into warm bowls and serve immediately.

COOK'S TIP

Brown stock is made with veal bones and shin of beef roasted with drippings in the oven for 40 minutes. Transfer the bones to a large pan and add sliced leeks, onion, celery, and carrots, a bouquet garni, white wine vinegar, and a thyme sprig, and cover with cold water. Simmer over a low heat for 3 hours. Strain and blot the fat from the surface of the stock with paper towels.

Veal & Mushroom Soup with Vermicelli

Serves 4

INGREDIENTS

1 pound veal, thinly sliced	pinch of mace	$^3/_4$ cup dried vermicelli
1 pound veal bones	5 ounces oyster and shiitake	1 tbsp cornstarch
5 cups water	mushrooms, roughly	3 tbsp milk
1 small onion	chopped	salt and pepper
6 peppercorns	$^5/_8$ cup heavy cream	
1 tsp cloves		

1 Put the veal, bones, and water into a large saucepan. Bring to a boil and lower the heat. Add the onion, peppercorns, cloves, and mace and simmer for about 3 hours, until the veal stock is reduced by one-third.

2 Strain the stock, skim off any fat on the surface with a slotted spoon, and pour the stock into a clean saucepan. Add the veal meat to the pan.

3 Add the mushrooms and cream, bring to a boil over a low heat, and simmer for 12 minutes. Meanwhile, cook the vermicelli in lightly salted boiling water until tender, but still firm to the bite. Drain and keep warm.

4 Mix together the cornstarch and milk to form a smooth paste. Stir the cornstarch paste into the soup to thicken. Season to taste and just before serving, add the vermicelli. Transfer the soup to a warm tureen and serve immediately.

COOK'S TIP

You can make this soup with the more inexpensive cuts of veal, such as breast or neck slices. These are lean and the long cooking time ensures that the meat is really tender.

Mussel & Potato Soup

Serves 4

INGREDIENTS

1 pound 10 ounces mussels	³/₄ cup dried conchigliette	TO GARNISH:
2 tbsp olive oil	1¹/₄ cups heavy cream	2 tbsp finely chopped fresh
7 tbsp unsalted butter	1 tbsp lemon juice	parsley
2 slices bacon, chopped	2 egg yolks	lemon wedges
1 onion, chopped	salt and pepper	
2 garlic cloves, crushed		
¹/₂ cup all-purpose flour		
1 pound potatoes, thinly sliced		

1 Debeard the mussels and scrub them under cold water for 5 minutes. Discard any mussels that do not close immediately when sharply tapped.

2 Bring a large pan of water to a boil, add the mussels, oil, and a little pepper and cook until the mussels open.

3 Drain the mussels, reserving the cooking liquid. Discard any mussels that are closed. Remove the mussels from their shells.

4 Melt the butter in a large saucepan and cook the bacon, onion, and garlic for 4 minutes. Carefully stir in the flour and then 5 cups of the reserved cooking liquid.

5 Add the potatoes to the pan and simmer for 5 minutes. Add the conchigliette and simmer for a further 10 minutes.

6 Add the cream and lemon juice, season to taste, then add the mussels to the pan.

7 Blend the egg yolks with 1-2 tbsp of the remaining cooking liquid, stir into the pan, and cook for 4 minutes.

8 Ladle the soup into warm soup bowls, garnish with the chopped fresh parsley and lemon wedges, and serve.

Italian Fish Soup

Serves 4

INGREDIENTS

4 tbsp butter
1 pound assorted fish fillets, such as red mullet and snapper
1 pound prepared seafood, such as squid and shrimp
8 ounces fresh crabmeat
1 large onion, sliced
1/4 cup all-purpose flour

5 cups fish stock (see Cook's Tip)
3/4 cup dried pasta shapes, such as ditalini or elbow macaroni
1 tbsp anchovy extract
grated rind and juice of 1 orange
1/4 cup dry sherry

1 1/4 cups heavy cream
salt and black pepper
crusty brown bread, to serve

1 Melt the butter in a large saucepan and cook the fish fillets, seafood, crabmeat, and onion over a low heat for 6 minutes.

2 Stir the flour into the mixture.

3 Gradually stir in the fish stock until the soup comes to a boil. Reduce the heat and simmer for 30 minutes.

4 Add the pasta to the saucepan and cook for a further 10 minutes.

5 Stir in the anchovy extract, orange rind, orange juice, sherry, and heavy cream. Season to taste with salt and pepper.

6 Heat the soup until completely warmed through then transfer to warm soup bowls and serve with crusty brown bread.

COOK'S TIP

The heads, tails, trimmings and bones of most non-oily fish can be used to make fish stock. Simmer 2 pounds fish pieces, including heads, in a large saucepan with 5/8 cup white wine, 1 chopped onion, 1 sliced carrot, 1 sliced celery stalk, 4 black peppercorns, 1 bouquet garni, and 7 1/2 cups water for 30 minutes, then strain.

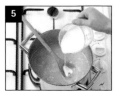

Spaghetti alla Carbonara

Serves 4

INGREDIENTS

15 ounces dried spaghetti
2 tbsp olive oil
1 large onion, thinly sliced
2 garlic cloves, chopped
6 slices bacon
2 tbsp butter

6 ounces mushrooms, thinly
sliced
1¼ cups heavy cream
3 eggs, beaten

1 cup freshly grated Parmesan
cheese, plus extra to serve
(optional)
salt and pepper
fresh sage sprigs, to garnish

1 Warm a large serving dish or bowl. Bring a large pan of lightly salted water to a boil. Add the spaghetti and 1 tbsp of the oil and cook until tender, but still firm to the bite. Drain, return to the pan, and keep warm.

2 Meanwhile, heat the remaining oil in a skillet over a medium heat. Add the onion and sauté until it is transparent. Add the garlic and bacon and fry until the bacon is crisp. Transfer to the warm plate.

3 Melt the butter in the skillet. Add the mushrooms and sauté, stirring occasionally, for 3-4 minutes. Return the bacon mixture to the pan. Cover and keep warm.

4 Mix together the cream, eggs, and cheese in a large bowl and then season to taste.

5 Working very quickly, tip the spaghetti into the bacon and mushroom mixture and pour in the eggs. Toss the spaghetti

quickly into the egg and cream mixture, using 2 forks, and serve immediately. If you wish, serve with extra grated Parmesan cheese.

COOK'S TIP

The key to success with this recipe is not to overcook the egg. That is why it is important to keep all the ingredients hot enough just to cook the egg and to work rapidly to avoid scrambling it.

Smoked Ham Linguini

Serves 4

INGREDIENTS

1 pound dried linguini	⁵⁄₈ cup Italian cheese sauce	salt and pepper
1 pound broccoli, broken into florets	(see Cook's Tip)	Italian bread, to serve
	8 ounces Italian smoked ham	

1 Bring a large pan of lightly salted water to a boil. Add the linguini and broccoli florets and cook for 10 minutes, until the linguini is tender, but still firm to the bite.

2 Drain the linguini and broccoli thoroughly, set aside, and keep warm.

3 Meanwhile, make the Italian cheese sauce (see Cook's Tip, right).

4 Using a sharp knife, cut the Italian smoked ham into thin strips. Toss the linguini, broccoli, and ham into the Italian cheese sauce and gently warm through over a very low heat.

5 Transfer the pasta mixture to a warm serving dish. Sprinkle with black pepper and serve with Italian bread.

COOK'S TIP

There are many types of Italian bread which would be suitable to serve with this dish. Ciabatta is made with olive oil and is available plain and with different ingredients, such as olives or sun-dried tomatoes.

COOK'S TIP

For Italian cheese sauce, melt 2 tbsp butter in a pan and stir in ¼ cup all-purpose flour. Cook, stirring, over a low heat until the roux is light in color and crumbly in texture. Stir in 1¼ cups hot milk. Cook, stirring, for 15 minutes until thick and smooth. Add a pinch of nutmeg, a pinch of dried thyme, 2 tbsp white wine vinegar, and season to taste. Stir in 3 tbsp heavy cream and mix. Stir in ½ cup grated Mozzarella cheese, ⅔ cup grated Parmesan cheese, 1 tsp English mustard, and 2 tbsp sour cream.

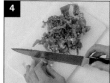

Chorizo & Mushrooms with a Spicy Vermicelli

Serves 6

INGREDIENTS

1¹/₂ pounds dried vermicelli
¹/₂ cup olive oil
2 garlic cloves
4¹/₂ ounces chorizo, sliced

8 ounces exotic mushrooms
3 fresh red chilies, chopped
2 tbsp freshly grated
Parmesan cheese

salt and pepper
10 anchovy fillets, to garnish

1 Bring a large saucepan of lightly salted water to a boil. Add the pasta and 1 tablespoon of the oil and cook until just tender, but still firm to the bite. Drain, transfer to a serving plate and keep warm.

2 Meanwhile heat the remaining oil in a large skillet. Add the garlic and fry for 1 minute. Add the chorizo and mushrooms and cook for about 4 minutes, then add the chopped chilies, and cook for 1 minute.

3 Pour the chorizo and mushroom mixture over the vermicelli and season with a little salt and pepper. Sprinkle with Parmesan, garnish with a lattice of anchovy fillets, and serve immediately.

VARIATION

Fresh sardines may be used instead of the chorizo. However, ensure that you gut and clean the sardines, removing the backbone, before using them.

COOK'S TIP

Always obtain exotic mushrooms from a reliable source and never pick them yourself. Many varieties of mushroom are now cultivated and most are indistinguishable from the exotic varieties. Mixed color oyster mushrooms have been used here, but you could also use chanterelles. However, remember that chanterelles tend to shrink during cooking, so you may need a larger quantity.

Pancetta & Pecorino Cakes on a Bed of Farfalle

Serves 4

INGREDIENTS

2 tbsp butter, plus extra
   for greasing
3¹/2 ounces pancetta, rind
   removed
2 cups self-rising flour
⁷/8 cup grated pecorino
   cheese

⁵/8 cup milk, plus extra for
   glazing
1 tsp Worcestershire sauce
1 tbsp ketchup
3¹/2 cups dried farfalle
1 tbsp olive oil
salt and black pepper

3 tbsp pesto (see page 12) or
   anchovy sauce (optional)
salad greens, to serve

1 Grease a cookie sheet with a little butter. Broil the pancetta until it is cooked. Allow the pancetta to cool, then chop it finely.

2 Sift together the flour and a pinch of salt into a mixing bowl. Add the butter and rub in with your fingertips. When the butter and flour have been thoroughly incorporated, add the pancetta and one-third of the grated cheese.

3 Mix together the milk, Worcestershire sauce, and ketchup and add to the dry ingredients, mixing to make a soft dough.

4 Roll out the dough on a lightly floured board to make a 7-inch round. Brush with a little milk to glaze and cut into 8 wedges.

5 Arrange the dough wedges on the prepared cookie sheet and sprinkle with the remaining cheese. Bake in a preheated oven at 400°F for 20 minutes.

6 Bring a pan of salted water to a boil. Add the farfalle and the oil and cook until just tender. Drain and transfer to a large serving dish. Top with the pancetta and pecorino cakes. Serve with the sauce of your choice and salad greens.

Orecchiette with Bacon & Tomatoes

Serves 4

INGREDIENTS

2 pounds small, sweet
   tomatoes
6 slices smoked bacon
4 tbsp butter
1 onion, chopped

1 garlic clove, crushed
4 fresh oregano sprigs,
   finely chopped
4 cups dried orecchiette
1 tbsp olive oil

salt and pepper
freshly grated Pecorino
   cheese, to serve

1 Blanch the tomatoes in boiling water. Drain, skin, and seed the tomatoes, then roughly chop the flesh. Chop the bacon into small pieces.

2 Melt the butter in a saucepan and fry the bacon until it is golden. Add the onion and garlic and fry over a medium heat until softened.

3 Add the tomatoes and oregano to the saucepan and season to taste. Lower the heat and simmer for 10-12 minutes.

4 Bring a pan of salted water to a boil. Add the orecchiette and oil and cook for 12 minutes, until just tender. Drain the pasta and transfer to a warm serving dish. Spoon the bacon and tomato sauce over the pasta, toss to coat, and serve with the cheese.

VARIATION

You could also use 1 pound spicy Italian sausages. Squeeze the meat out of the skins and add to the pan in step 2 instead of the bacon.

COOK'S TIP

For an authentic Italian flavor use pancetta, rather than ordinary bacon. This kind of bacon is streaked with fat and adds rich undertones of flavor to many traditional dishes. It is available both smoked and unsmoked, and can be bought in a single, large piece or cut into slices. You can buy it in some supermarkets and all Italian delicatessens.

Creamed Veal Kidneys with Penne & Pesto Sauce

Serves 4

INGREDIENTS

5 tbsp butter

12 veal kidneys, trimmed and thinly sliced

6 ounces button mushrooms, sliced

1 tsp English mustard

pinch of freshly grated ginger root

2 tbsp dry sherry

5/8 cup heavy cream

2 tbsp pesto sauce (see page 12)

14 ounces dried penne

1 tbsp olive oil

salt and pepper

4 slices of hot toast cut into triangles

fresh parsley sprigs, to garnish

1 Melt the butter in a large skillet and fry the kidneys over a low heat for 4 minutes. Transfer the kidneys to an ovenproof dish and keep warm.

2 Add the mushrooms to the skillet, and cook for about 2 minutes.

3 Add the mustard and ginger to the pan and season to taste. Cook for 2 minutes, then add the sherry, cream, and pesto sauce. Cook for an additional 3 minutes, then pour the sauce over the kidneys. Bake in a preheated oven at 375°F for 10 minutes.

4 Meanwhile, bring a large pan of lightly salted water to a boil. Add the penne and the oil and cook until just tender, but still firm to the bite. Drain the pasta and transfer to a warm serving dish.

5 Top the pasta with the kidneys in the pesto sauce. Place triangles of warm toast around the kidneys, garnish with fresh parsley and serve.

COOK'S TIP

Store the pesto sauce in an airtight container for up to a week in the refrigerator, or freeze (before adding the Parmesan) for 3 months.

Marinated Eggplant on a Bed of Linguine

Serves 4

INGREDIENTS

⁵/₈ cup vegetable stock
⁵/₈ cup white wine vinegar
2 tsp balsamic vinegar
3 tbsp olive oil
fresh oregano sprig
1 pound eggplant, peeled and
　thinly sliced
14 ounces dried linguine

MARINADE:
2 tbsp extra virgin oil
2 garlic cloves, crushed
2 tbsp chopped fresh oregano
2 tbsp finely chopped
　roasted almonds
2 tbsp diced red bell pepper
2 tbsp lime juice

grated rind and juice of
　1 orange
salt and pepper

1 Put the vegetable stock, wine vinegar, and balsamic vinegar into a saucepan and bring to a boil over a low heat. Add 2 tsp of the olive oil and the sprig of oregano and simmer gently for about 1 minute.

2 Add the eggplant slices to the saucepan, remove from the heat and set aside for 10 minutes.

3 Meanwhile, make the marinade. Combine the olive oil, garlic, fresh oregano, almonds, bell pepper, lime juice, orange rind, and juice in a large bowl and season to taste with salt and pepper.

4 Remove the eggplant from the saucepan and drain well. Add the eggplant slices to the marinade, mixing well, and

set aside in the refrigerator for about 12 hours.

5 Bring a pan of lightly salted water to a boil. Add half the remaining oil and the linguine and cook until just tender. Drain the pasta and toss with the remaining oil. Arrange the pasta on a serving plate with the eggplant slices and the marinade and serve.

Spinach & Ricotta Shells

Serves 4

INGREDIENTS

14 ounces dried lumache
  rigate grande
5 tbsp olive oil
1 cup fresh white
  breadcrumbs
$1/2$ cup milk

$10^1/2$ ounces frozen spinach,
  thawed and drained
1 cup ricotta cheese
pinch of freshly grated
  nutmeg

14 ounce can chopped
  tomatoes, drained
1 garlic clove, crushed
salt and pepper

1 Bring a large saucepan of lightly salted water to a boil. Add the lumache and 1 tbsp of the olive oil and cook until just tender, but still firm to the bite. Drain the pasta, rinse under cold water, and set aside.

2 Put the breadcrumbs, milk, and 3 tbsp of the remaining olive oil in a food processor and work to combine.

3 Add the spinach and ricotta cheese to the food processor and work to a smooth mixture. Transfer to a bowl, stir in the nutmeg, and season with salt and pepper to taste.

4 Mix together the tomatoes, garlic, and remaining oil and spoon the mixture into the base of an ovenproof dish.

5 Using a teaspoon, fill the lumache with the spinach and ricotta mixture and arrange on top of the tomato mixture in the dish.

Cover and bake in a preheated oven at 350°F for 20 minutes. Serve hot.

COOK'S TIP

Ricotta is a creamy Italian cheese traditionally made from ewes' milk whey. It is soft and white, with a smooth texture and a slightly sweet flavor. It should be used within 2–3 days of purchase.

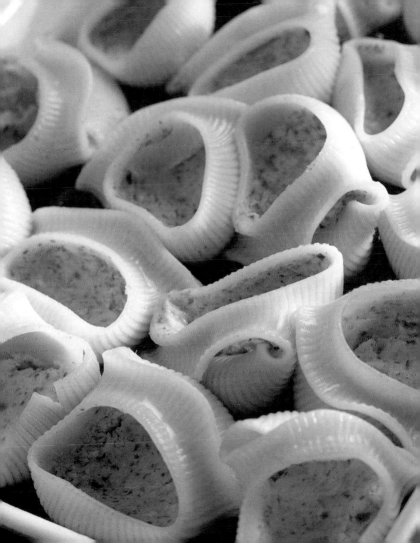

Rotelle with Spicy Italian Sauce

Serves 4

INGREDIENTS

$2^7/8$ cup Italian red wine
   sauce (see Cook's Tip,
   bottom right)

5 tbsp olive oil
3 garlic cloves, crushed
2 fresh red chilies, chopped
1 green chili, chopped

$3^1/2$ cups dried rotelle
salt and pepper
warm Italian bread, to serve

1 Make the Italian Red Wine Sauce (see Cook's Tip, right).

2 Heat 4 tbsp of the oil in a saucepan. Add the garlic and chilies and sauté for 3 minutes.

3 Stir in the Italian red wine sauce, season to taste, and simmer gently for about 20 minutes.

4 Bring a large pan of lightly salted water to a boil. Add the rotelle and the remaining oil and cook for 8 minutes, until just tender. Drain the pasta.

5 Toss the rotelle in the spicy sauce, transfer to a warm dish, and serve with warm Italian bread.

COOK'S TIP

Take care when using fresh chilies as they can burn your skin. Handle them as little as possible—wear rubber gloves if necessary. Wash your hands thoroughly afterward, and don't touch your face or eyes before you have washed your hands. Remove chili seeds before chopping the chilies, as they are the hottest part.

COOK'S TIP

To make Italian red wine sauce, first make a demi-glace sauce by combining $5/8$ cup each brown stock (see page 28) and espagnole sauce (see page 14), cook for 10 minutes, and strain. Mix $1/2$ cup red wine, 2 tbsp red wine vinegar, 4 tbsp chopped shallots, 1 bay leaf and 1 thyme sprig in a small pan. Bring to a boil and reduce by about three-quarters. Add the demi-glace sauce to the pan and simmer for about 20 minutes. Season to taste and strain.

Tricolor Timballini

Serves 4

INGREDIENTS

1 tbsp butter, softened
1 cup dried white
    breadcrumbs
6 ounces dried tricolor
    spaghetti, broken into
    2-inch lengths
3 tbsp olive oil

1 egg yolk
1 cup grated Swiss cheese
1$\frac{1}{4}$ cups Béchamel sauce (see
    page 166)
1 onion, finely chopped
1 bay leaf
$\frac{5}{8}$ cup dry white wine

$\frac{5}{8}$ cup sieved tomatoes
1 tbsp tomato paste
salt and pepper
fresh basil leaves, to garnish

1 Grease four ¾ cup molds or ramekins with the butter. Evenly coat the insides with half the breadcrumbs.

2 Bring a saucepan of lightly salted water to a boil. Add the spaghetti and 1 tbsp of the oil and cook until just tender. Drain and transfer to a mixing bowl.

3 Add the egg yolk and cheese to the pasta and season. Mix in the béchamel sauce. Spoon the mixture into the ramekins and sprinkle with the remaining breadcrumbs.

4 Stand the ramekins on a cookie sheet and bake in a preheated oven at 425°F for 20 minutes. Set aside for 10 minutes.

5 Meanwhile, make the sauce. Heat the remaining oil in a pan and gently sauté the onion and bay leaf for 2-3 minutes.

6 Stir in the wine, sieved tomatoes, and tomato paste and season. Simmer for 20 minutes, until thickened. Remove and discard the bay leaf.

7 Turn the timballini out onto individual serving plates, garnish with the basil leaves, and serve with the tomato sauce.

Tagliarini with Gorgonzola

Serves 4

INGREDIENTS

2 tbsp butter
8 ounces Gorgonzola cheese,
    roughly crumbled
5/8 cup heavy cream

2 tbsp dry white wine
1 tsp cornstarch
4 fresh sage sprigs, finely
    chopped
14 ounces dried tagliarini

2 tbsp olive oil
salt and white pepper

1 Melt the butter in a
saucepan, stir in 6
ounces of the Gorgonzola
cheese and melt, over a low
heat, for about 2 minutes.

2 Add the cream, wine,
and cornstarch to the
pan and beat with a whisk
until fully incorporated.

3 Stir in the sage and
season to taste with salt
and white pepper. Bring to
a boil over a low heat,
whisking constantly, until
the sauce thickens.
Remove from the heat
and set aside.

4 Bring a large pan of
lightly salted water to a
boil. Add the tagliarini and
1 tbsp of the olive oil.
Cook the pasta for
12–14 minutes, or until just
tender, drain and toss in the
remaining oil. Transfer the
pasta to a serving dish and
keep warm.

5 Reheat the sauce over a
low heat, whisking
constantly. Spoon the
Gorgonzola sauce over the
tagliarini, generously
sprinkle with the remaining
crumbled cheese, and serve
immediately.

COOK'S TIP

*Gorgonzola is one of the
world's oldest veined cheeses
and, arguably, its finest.
Always check that it is
creamy yellow with delicate
green veining. Avoid hard
or discolored cheese. It
should have a rich, piquant
aroma, not a bitter smell. If
you find Gorgonzola too
strong or rich, substitute a
milder blue cheese.*

Gnocchi Piemontese

Serves 4

INGREDIENTS

1 pound warm mashed potato	$^5/_8$ cup espagnole sauce	salt and pepper
$^5/_8$ cup self-rising flour	(see page 14)	
1 egg	4 tbsp butter	
2 egg yolks	2 cups freshly grated	
1 tbsp olive oil	Parmesan cheese	

1 Combine the mashed potato and flour in a bowl. Add the egg and egg yolks, season well, and mix together to form a dough.

2 Break off pieces of the dough and roll them between the palms of your hands to form small balls the size of a walnut. Flatten the balls with a fork into the shape of small circles.

3 Bring a large pan of lightly salted water to a boil. Add the gnocchi and olive oil and poach for 10 minutes.

4 Mix the espagnole sauce (see page 14) and the butter in a large saucepan over a gentle heat. Gradually blend in the grated Parmesan cheese.

5 Remove the gnocchi from the pan and toss in the sauce, transfer to 4 individual serving plates, and serve immediately.

COOK'S TIP

This dish also makes an excellent main meal with a crisp salad.

VARIATION

These gnocchi would also taste delicious with a tomato sauce, in Trentino-style. Mix together 1 cup finely chopped sun-dried tomatoes, 1 finely sliced celery stalk, 1 crushed garlic clove, and 6 tbsp red wine in a pan. Cook over a low heat for 15–20 minutes. Stir in 8 skinned, chopped, Italian plum tomatoes, season to taste with salt and pepper, and simmer over a low heat for a further 10 minutes.

Pasta Omelet

Serves 2

INGREDIENTS

4 tbsp olive oil
1 small onion, chopped
1 fennel bulb, thinly sliced
4¹/2 ounces potato, diced
1 garlic clove, chopped
4 eggs

1 tbsp chopped fresh parsley
pinch of chili powder
3¹/2 ounces cooked short
   pasta
2 tbsp stuffed green olives,
   halved

salt and pepper
fresh marjoram sprigs, to
   garnish
tomato salad, to serve

1 Heat half the oil in a skillet over a low heat and cook the onion, fennel, and potato, stirring, for 8-10 minutes, until the potato is just tender.

2 Add the garlic and fry for 1 minute. Remove the pan from the heat, transfer the vegetables to a plate, and set aside.

3 Beat the eggs until they are frothy. Stir in the parsley and season with salt, pepper, and a pinch of chili powder.

4 Heat 1 tablespoon of the remaining oil in a clean skillet. Add half of the egg mixture to the pan, then add the cooked vegetables, pasta, and half of the olives. Pour in the remaining egg mixture and cook until the sides begin to set.

5 Lift up the edges of the omelet with a spatula to allow the uncooked egg to spread underneath. Cook until the underside of the omelet is a light golden brown color.

6 Slide the omelet out of the pan onto a plate. Wipe the pan with paper towels and heat the remaining oil. Invert the omelet into the pan and cook until the other side is golden brown.

7 Slide the omelet onto a warmed serving dish and garnish with the remaining olives and the marjoram. Serve cut into wedges, with a tomato salad.

Spaghetti with Ricotta Cheese

Serves 4

INGREDIENTS

12 ounces dried spaghetti
3 tbsp olive oil
3 tbsp butter
2 tbsp chopped fresh parsley
1 cup freshly ground almonds
$^1/_2$ cup ricotta cheese

pinch of grated nutmeg
pinch of ground cinnamon
$^5/_8$ cup unsweetened yogurt
$^1/_2$ cup hot chicken stock
1 tbsp pine nuts

salt and pepper
fresh parsley sprigs, to garnish

1 Bring a large pan of lightly salted water to a boil. Add the spaghetti and 1 tbsp of the oil and cook until tender, but still firm to the bite.

2 Drain the pasta, return to the pan, and toss with the butter and chopped parsley. Set aside and keep warm.

3 To make the sauce, mix together the ground almonds, ricotta cheese, nutmeg, cinnamon, and unsweetened yogurt over a low heat to form a thick paste. Stir in the remaining oil, then gradually stir in the hot chicken stock, until smooth. Season the sauce with black pepper to taste.

4 Transfer the spaghetti to a warm serving dish, pour the sauce on top, and toss together well (see Cook's Tip). Sprinkle with the pine nuts, garnish with the fresh parsley, and serve the spaghetti warm.

COOK'S TIP

Use two large forks to toss spaghetti or other long pasta, so that it is thoroughly coated with the sauce. Special spaghetti forks are available from some cookware departments and kitchen stores. Holding one fork in each hand, gently ease the prongs under the pasta on each side and lift them toward the center. Continue until the pasta is completely coated.

Gnocchi Romana

Serves 4

INGREDIENTS

3¹/8 cups milk	1¹/4 cups cream of wheat	salt and pepper
pinch of freshly grated nutmeg	1¹/2 cups grated Parmesan cheese	fresh basil sprigs, to garnish
6 tbsp butter, plus extra for greasing	2 eggs, beaten	
	¹/2 cup grated Swiss cheese	

1 Pour the milk into a saucepan and bring to a boil. Remove from the heat and stir in the nutmeg, 2 tbsp of the butter, and salt and pepper to taste.

2 Gradually stir the semolina into the milk, whisking to prevent lumps forming, and return the pan to a low heat. Simmer, stirring constantly, for about 10 minutes, until the mixture is very thick.

3 Beat ⅔ cup of the Parmesan into the semolina mixture, then

beat in the eggs. Continue beating until smooth. Set aside to cool slightly.

4 Spread out the semonlina mixture in an even layer on a sheet of waxed paper or in a large, oiled baking pan. Smooth the surface with a damp spatula—it should be about ½-inch thick. Set aside to cool completely, then leave to chill for 1 hour.

5 Once chilled, cut out rounds of gnocchi, measuring about 1½ inches in diameter.

6 Grease a shallow ovenproof dish or 4 individual dishes. Lay the gnocchi trimmings in the base of the dish or dishes and cover with overlapping rounds of gnocchi.

7 Melt the remaining butter and drizzle over the gnocchi. Sprinkle with the remaining Parmesan and the Swiss cheese.

8 Bake in a preheated oven at 400°F for 25-30 minutes, until the top is crisp and golden brown. Garnish and serve.

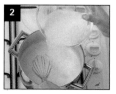

Three Cheese Bake

Serves 4

INGREDIENTS

butter, for greasing
14 ounces dried penne
1 tbsp olive oil
2 eggs, beaten
1¹/₂ cups ricotta cheese
4 fresh basil sprigs

1 cup grated mozzarella or
 halloumi cheese
4 tbsp freshly grated
 Parmesan cheese
salt and black pepper

fresh basil leaves (optional), to
 garnish

1 Lightly grease an ovenproof dish.

2 Bring a large pan of lightly salted water to a boil. Add the penne and olive oil and cook until just tender, but still firm to the bite. Drain the pasta, set aside, and keep warm.

3 Beat the eggs into the ricotta cheese and season to taste with salt and pepper.

4 Spoon half of the penne into the base of the dish

and cover with half of the basil leaves.

5 Spoon over half of the ricotta cheese mixture. Sprinkle with the mozzarella or halloumi cheese and then top with the remaining basil leaves. Cover with the remaining penne and then spoon over the remaining ricotta cheese mixture. Lightly sprinkle with the grated Parmesan cheese.

6 Bake in a preheated oven at 375°F for

30–40 minutes, until golden brown and the cheese topping is bubbling.

7 Garnish with basil leaves, if desired, and serve hot.

VARIATION

Try substituting smoked Bavarian cheese for the mozzarella or halloumi and grated Cheddar cheese for the Parmesan, for a slightly different but just as delicious flavor.

Baked Rigatoni Filled with Tuna & Ricotta Cheese

Serves 4

INGREDIENTS

butter, for greasing	1 cup ricotta cheese	4 ounces sun-dried tomatoes,
1 pound dried rigatoni	$^1/_2$ cup heavy cream	drained and sliced
1 tbsp olive oil	$2^2/_3$ cups grated Parmesan	salt and black pepper
7 ounce can flaked tuna,	cheese	
drained		

1 Lightly grease an ovenproof dish with butter.

2 Bring a large saucepan of lightly salted water to a boil. Add the rigatoni and olive oil and cook until just tender, but still firm to the bite. Drain the pasta and set aside until cool enough to handle.

3 In a bowl, mix together the tuna and ricotta cheese to form a soft paste. Spoon the mixture into a piping bag and use to fill the rigatoni. Arrange the filled pasta tubes side by side in the prepared ovenproof dish.

4 To make the sauce, mix the cream and Parmesan cheese, and season. Spoon the sauce over the rigatoni and top with the sun-dried tomatoes arranged in a criss-cross pattern. Bake in a preheated oven at 400°F for 20 minutes. Serve immediately.

VARIATION

For a vegetarian alternative of this recipe, simply substitute a mixture of pitted and chopped black olives and chopped walnuts for the tuna. Follow exactly the same cooking method.

Spaghetti with Anchovy & Pesto Sauce

Serves 4

INGREDIENTS

$^3/_8$ cup olive oil

2 garlic cloves, crushed

2 ounce can anchovy fillets, drained

1 pound dried spaghetti

2 ounces pesto sauce (see page 12)

2 tbsp finely chopped fresh oregano

1 cup grated Parmesan cheese, plus extra for serving (optional)

salt and pepper

2 fresh oregano sprigs, to garnish

1 Reserve 1 tbsp of the oil and heat the remainder in a small saucepan. Add the garlic and fry for 3 minutes.

2 Lower the heat, stir in the anchovies, and cook, stirring occasionally, until the anchovies have disintegrated.

3 Bring a large saucepan of lightly salted water to a boil. Add the spaghetti and the remaining olive oil and cook until just tender.

4 Add the pesto sauce (see page 12) and chopped fresh oregano to the anchovy mixture and then season with black pepper to taste.

5 Drain the spaghetti and transfer to a warm serving dish. Pour over the pesto sauce and then sprinkle over the grated Parmesan cheese, if using.

6 Garnish with oregano sprigs and serve with extra cheese, if using.

VARIATION

For a vegetarian version of this recipe, simply substitute drained sun-dried tomatoes for the anchovy fillets.

COOK'S TIP

If you find canned anchovies much too salty, soak them in a saucer of milk for 5 minutes, drain, and pat dry with paper towels before using them.

Fettuccine with Anchovy & Spinach Sauce

Serves 4

INGREDIENTS

2 pounds fresh, young spinach leaves	6 tbsp olive oil	8 canned anchovy fillets, drained and chopped
14 ounces dried fettuccine	3 tbsp pine nuts	salt
	3 garlic cloves, crushed	

1 Trim off any tough spinach stalks. Rinse the spinach leaves and place them in a large saucepan with only the water that is clinging to them after washing. Cover and cook over a high heat, shaking the pan from time, until the spinach has wilted, but retains its color. Drain well, set aside and keep warm.

2 Bring a large saucepan of lightly salted water to a boil. Add the fettuccine and 1 tbsp of the oil and cook until it is just tender, but still firm to the bite.

3 Heat 4 tbsp of the remaining olive oil in a saucepan. Add the pine nuts and fry until golden. Remove from the pan and set aside.

4 Add the garlic to the pan and fry until golden. Add the anchovies and stir in the spinach. Cook, stirring, for 2-3 minutes, until heated through. Return the pine nuts to the pan, stirring until well combined.

5 Drain the fettuccine, toss in the remaining olive oil, and transfer to a warm serving dish. Spoon the anchovy and spinach sauce over the fettuccine, toss lightly, and serve immediately.

COOK'S TIP

If you are in a hurry, you can use frozen spinach. Thaw and drain it thoroughly, pressing out as much moisture as possible. Cut the leaves into strips and add to the dish with the anchovies in step 4.

Penne with Muscoli Fritti nell' Olio

Serves 4-6

INGREDIENTS

3½ cups dried penne
½ cup olive oil
1 pound mussels, cooked
   and shelled
1 tsp sea salt

⅔ cup all-purpose flour
3½ ounces sun-dried
   tomatoes, sliced
salt and pepper

TO GARNISH:
1 lemon, thinly sliced
basil leaves

1 Bring a large pan of lightly salted water to a boil. Add the penne and 1 tbsp of the olive oil and cook until the pasta is just tender, but still firm to the bite.

2 Drain the pasta and place in a serving dish. Set aside and keep warm.

3 Lightly sprinkle the mussels with the sea salt. Season the flour with salt and pepper, sprinkle into a bowl, and toss the mussels in the flour until well coated.

4 Heat the remaining oil in a skillet and fry the mussels, stirring frequently, until golden brown.

5 Toss the mussels with the penne and sprinkle with the sun-dried tomatoes. Garnish with lemon slices and basil leaves and serve.

VARIATION

You could substitute clams for the mussels. If using fresh clams, try smaller varieties, such as Venus.

COOK'S TIP

Sun-dried tomatoes have been used in Mediterranean countries for a long time, but have become popular elsewhere only quite recently. They are dried and then preserved in oil. They have a concentrated, almost roasted flavor and a dense texture. They should be drained and chopped or sliced before using.

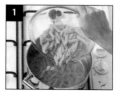

Meat & Poultry

Pasta and meat or poultry is a classic combination. Dishes range from easy, economic mid-week suppers to sophisticated and elegant meals for special occasions. The recipes in this chapter include many family favorites, such as Spaghetti Bolognese, Fresh Spaghetti with Italian Meatballs in Tomato Sauce, Lasagne Verde, and Stuffed Cannelloni. There are also some exciting variations on traditional themes, such as Sicilian Spaghetti, Beef & Pasta Bake, and Stir-fried Pork with Pasta & Vegetables. Finally, there is a superb collection of mouthwatering original recipes. Why not try Fettuccine with Fillet of Veal & Pink Grapefruit in a Rose Petal Butter Sauce, Orecchioni with Pork in Cream Sauce, garnished with Quail Eggs, Chicken & Lobster on a Bed of Penne, or Rigatoni & Pesto Baked Partridge? You will be astonished at how quickly and easily you can prepare these gourmet dishes.

Spaghetti Bolognese

Serves 4

INGREDIENTS

3 tbsp olive oil
2 garlic cloves, crushed
1 large onion, finely chopped
1 carrot, diced
2 cups lean ground beef, veal,
  or chicken

3 ounces chicken livers,
  finely chopped
3¹/2 ounces lean prosciutto,
  diced
⁵/8 cup Marsala
10 ounce can chopped
  plum tomatoes

1 tbsp chopped fresh basil
  leaves
2 tbsp tomato paste
salt and pepper
1 pound dried spaghetti

1 Heat 2 tbsp of the olive oil in a large saucepan. Add the garlic, onion, and carrot and sauté for 6 minutes.

2 Add the ground beef, veal, or chicken, the chicken livers, and prosciutto to the pan and cook over a medium heat, stirring occasionally, for 12 minutes, until well browned.

3 Stir in the Marsala, tomatoes, basil, and tomato paste and cook for 4 minutes. Season to taste with salt and pepper. Cover and simmer for about 30 minutes.

4 Remove the lid from the pan, stir, and simmer for a further 15 minutes.

5 Meanwhile, bring a large pan of lightly salted water to a boil. Add the spaghetti and the remaining oil and cook for about 12 minutes, until tender, but still firm to the bite. Drain and transfer to a serving dish. Pour the sauce over the pasta, toss, and serve hot.

VARIATION

Chicken livers are an essential ingredient in a classic Bolognese sauce to which they add richness. However, if you prefer not to use them, you can substitute the same quantity of ground beef.

Creamed Strips of Sirloin with Rigatoni

Serves 4

INGREDIENTS

6 tbsp butter
1 pound sirloin steak, trimmed
 and cut into thin strips
6 ounces button mushrooms,
 sliced
1 tsp mustard
pinch of freshly grated ginger
 root

2 tbsp dry sherry
$5/8$ cup heavy cream
salt and pepper
4 slices hot toast, cut into
 triangles, to serve

PASTA:
1 pound dried rigatoni
2 tbsp olive oil
2 fresh basil sprigs
8 tbsp butter

1 Preheat the oven to 375°F. Melt the butter in a large skillet and gently fry the steak, stirring frequently, for 6 minutes. Transfer to an ovenproof dish and keep warm.

2 Add the mushrooms to the remaining juices in the skillet and cook for 2–3 minutes. Add the mustard, ginger, and salt and pepper to taste. Cook for about 2 minutes, then add the sherry and cream. Cook for an additional 3 minutes, then pour the cream sauce over the steak.

3 Bake the steak and cream mixture in the preheated oven for 10 minutes.

4 Bring a large saucepan of lightly salted water to a boil. Add the rigatoni, olive oil, and 1 basil sprig and boil rapidly for 10 minutes, until tender but still firm to the bite. Drain the pasta and transfer to a warm serving plate. Toss the pasta with the butter and garnish with the remaining basil sprig.

5 Serve the steak with the pasta and triangles of warm toast. Serve the rigatoni separately.

Fresh Spaghetti with Italian Meatballs in Tomato Sauce

Serves 4

INGREDIENTS

2¹/₂ cups brown breadcrumbs
⁵/₈ cup milk
2 tbsp butter
¹/₄ cup whole-wheat flour
⁷/₈ cup beef stock
14 ounce can chopped
  tomatoes
2 tbsp tomato paste

1 tsp sugar
1 tbsp finely chopped fresh
  tarragon
1 large onion, chopped
4 cups ground steak
1 tsp paprika
4 tbsp olive oil
1 pound fresh spaghetti

salt and pepper
fresh tarragon sprigs, to
  garnish

1 Soak the breadcrumbs in the milk for 30 minutes.

2 Melt half the butter in a pan. Stir in the flour and cook for 2 minutes. Gradually stir in the beef stock and cook, stirring constantly, for a further 5 minutes. Add the tomatoes, tomato paste, sugar, and tarragon. Season well and simmer for 25 minutes.

3 Mix the onion, steak, and paprika into the breadcrumbs and season. Shape into 14 meatballs.

4 Heat the oil and remaining butter in a skillet and fry the meatballs until brown all over. Place them in a deep casserole, pour the tomato sauce over the meatballs, cover, and bake in a preheated oven at 350°F for 25 minutes.

5 Cook the spaghetti in a pan of lightly salted boiling water for about 2–3 minutes, until tender, but still firm to the bite.

6 Meanwhile, remove the meatballs from the oven and allow them to cool for 3 minutes. Serve the meatballs and their sauce with the spaghetti, garnished with tarragon sprigs.

Layered Meat Loaf

Serves 6

INGREDIENTS

2 tbsp butter, plus extra for greasing	1 tbsp lemon juice	6 ounces bacon
1 small onion, finely chopped	1/2 tsp grated lemon rind	salt and pepper
1 small red bell pepper, cored, seeded, and chopped	2 tbsp chopped fresh parsley	salad greens, to garnish
1 garlic clove, chopped	3/4 cup dried short pasta, such as fusilli	
4 cups ground beef	1 tbsp olive oil	
1/2 cup white breadcrumbs	1 cup Italian cheese sauce (see page 38)	
1/2 tsp cayenne pepper	4 bay leaves	

1 Preheat the oven to 350°F. Melt the butter in a pan and sauté the onion and bell pepper for 3 minutes. Stir in the garlic and cook for 1 minute.

2 Put the meat into a bowl and mash with a wooden spoon until sticky. Add the onion mixture, breadcrumbs, cayenne pepper, lemon juice, lemon rind, and parsley. Season and set aside.

3 Bring a pan of salted water to a boil. Add the pasta and oil and cook for 8–10 minutes, until almost tender. Drain and stir into the Italian cheese sauce.

4 Grease a 2-pound loaf pan and arrange the bay leaves in the base. Stretch the bacon slices and line the base and sides of the pan with them. Spoon in half the meat mixture and smooth the surface.

Cover with the pasta mixed with Italian cheese sauce, then spoon in the remaining meat mixture. Level the top and cover with foil.

5 Bake the meat loaf for 1 hour, or until the juices run clear when a skewer is inserted in the center. Pour off any excess fat and turn out the loaf onto a warm serving dish. Garnish with salad greens.

Egg Noodles with Beef

Serves 4

INGREDIENTS

10 ounces egg noodles
3 tbsp walnut oil
1-inch piece fresh ginger root,
    cut into thin strips
5 scallions, finely shredded
2 garlic cloves, finely chopped
1 red bell pepper, cored,
    seeded, and thinly sliced

3^1/$_2$ ounces button
    mushrooms, thinly sliced
12 ounces fillet steak, cut into
    thin strips
1 tbsp cornstarch
5 tbsp dry sherry
3 tbsp soy sauce
1 tsp soft brown sugar

1 cup bean sprouts
1 tbsp sesame oil
salt and pepper
scallion strips, to garnish

1 Bring a large pan of water to a boil. Add the noodles and cook according to the instructions on the packet. Drain the noodles, set aside, and keep warm.

2 Heat the walnut oil in a preheated wok and stir-fry the ginger, scallions, and garlic for 45 seconds. Add the bell pepper, mushrooms, and steak and stir-fry for 4 minutes. Season to taste.

3 Mix together the cornstarch, sherry, and soy sauce in a small bowl to form a paste, and pour into the wok. Sprinkle in the brown sugar and stir-fry all of the ingredients for 2 minutes longer.

4 Add the bean sprouts, drained noodles, and sesame oil to the wok, stir and toss together for 1 minute. Transfer to serving plates, garnish with strips of scallion and serve.

COOK'S TIP

If you do not have a wok, you could prepare this dish in a skillet. However, a wok is preferable, as the round base ensures an even distribution of heat and it is easier to keep stirring and tossing the contents when stir-frying.

Tagliarini with Meatballs in Red Wine & Oyster Mushroom Sauce

Serves 4

INGREDIENTS

2 cups white breadcrumbs
⁵/₈ cup milk
2 tbsp butter
9 tbsp olive oil
3 cups sliced
   oyster mushrooms
¹/₄ cup whole-wheat flour
⁷/₈ cup beef stock
⁵/₈ cup red wine

4 tomatoes, skinned and
   chopped
1 tbsp tomato paste
1 tsp brown sugar
1 tbsp finely chopped fresh
   basil
12 shallots, chopped
4 cups ground steak
1 tsp paprika

1 pound dried egg tagliarini
salt and pepper
fresh basil sprigs, to garnish

1 Soak the breadcrumbs in the milk for 30 minutes.

2 Sauté the mushrooms in half the butter and 4 tbsp of the oil for 4 minutes. Stir in the flour. Add the stock and wine and simmer for 15 minutes. Add the tomatoes, tomato paste, sugar, and basil and simmer for 30 minutes.

3 Mix the shallots, steak, and paprika with the breadcrumbs and season. Shape into 14 meatballs.

4 Heat 4 tbsp of the remaining oil and the remaining butter in a skillet. Fry the meatballs until brown all over. Transfer to a deep casserole, pour in the red wine and the mushroom sauce, cover, and

bake in a preheated oven at 350°F for 30 minutes.

5 Bring a pan of salted water to a boil. Add the pasta and the remaining oil and cook until tender. Drain and transfer to a serving dish. Pour the meatballs and sauce onto the pasta, garnish with the basil sprigs, and serve.

Sicilian Spaghetti

Serves 4

INGREDIENTS

⁵/₈ cup olive oil, plus extra for
   brushing
2 eggplants
3 cups ground beef
1 onion, chopped
2 garlic cloves, crushed
2 tbsp tomato paste

14 ounce can chopped
   tomatoes
1 tsp Worcestershire sauce
1 tsp chopped fresh marjoram
   or oregano or ¹/₂ tsp dried
   marjoram or oregano
¹/₂ cup pitted black olives,
   sliced

1 green, red, or yellow bell
   pepper, cored, seeded, and
   chopped
6 ounces dried spaghetti
1 cup freshly grated Parmesan
   cheese
salt and pepper

1 Brush an 8-inch loose-based round cake pan with oil, line the base with baking parchment, and brush with oil.

2 Slice the eggplant. Heat a little olive oil in a pan and fry the eggplant until browned on both sides. Drain on paper towels.

3 Put the beef, onion, and garlic in a saucepan and cook, stirring until browned. Add the

tomato paste, tomatoes, Worcestershire sauce, marjoram or oregano, and salt and pepper. Simmer, stirring occasionally, for 10 minutes. Add the olives and bell pepper and cook for 10 minutes longer.

4 Bring a pan of salted water to a boil. Add the spaghetti and 1 tablespoon of olive oil and cook until tender, but still firm to the bite. Drain and turn the spaghetti into a bowl. Add

the meat mixture and cheese and toss together.

5 Arrange eggplant slices over the base and up the sides of the cake pan. Add the spaghetti and then cover with the rest of the eggplant slices. Bake in a preheated oven at 400°F for 40 minutes. Let stand for 5 minutes, then invert onto a serving dish. Discard the baking parchment and serve immediately.

Beef & Pasta Bake

Serves 4

INGREDIENTS

2 pounds steak, cut into cubes
about ¹/₂ cup beef stock
1 pound dried macaroni
1¹/₄ cups heavy cream
¹/₂ tsp garam masala
salt
fresh cilantro, to garnish
nan bread, to serve

KORMA PASTE:
¹/₂ cup blanched almonds
6 garlic cloves
1-inch piece fresh ginger root,
    coarsely chopped
6 tbsp beef stock
1 tsp ground cardamom
4 cloves, crushed
1 tsp cinnamon

2 large onions, chopped
1 tsp coriander seeds
2 tsp ground cumin seeds
pinch of cayenne pepper
6 tbsp of sunflower oil

1 Grind the almonds finely using a pestle and mortar. Put the ground almonds and the rest of the korma paste ingredients into a food processor or blender and process well to make a very smooth paste.

2 Put the steak in a shallow dish and spoon over the korma paste, turning to coat the steak well. Marinate in the refrigerator for 6 hours.

3 Transfer the steak to a large saucepan, and simmer gently, adding a little beef stock if required, for 35 minutes.

4 Bring a large saucepan of salted water to a boil. Add the macaroni and cook for 10 minutes, until tender, but still firm to the touch. Drain the pasta and transfer to a deep casserole. Add the steak, heavy cream, and garam masala.

5 Bake in a preheated oven at 400°F for 30 minutes. Remove from the oven and allow to stand for 10 minutes. Garnish with fresh cilantro and serve with nan bread.

VARIATION

You could also make this dish using diced chicken and chicken stock, instead of steak and beef stock.

Lasagne Verde

Serves 4–6

INGREDIENTS

butter, for greasing
14 sheets precooked lasagne
3³/₄ cups Béchamel sauce (see page 166)
³/₄ cup grated mozzarella cheese
fresh basil (optional), to garnish

MEAT SAUCE:
¹/₈ cup olive oil
4 cups ground beef
1 large onion, chopped
1 celery stalk, diced
4 cloves garlic, crushed
¹/₄ cup all-purpose flour
1¹/₄ cups beef stock
⁵/₈ cup red wine

1 tbsp chopped fresh parsley
1 tsp chopped fresh marjoram
1 tsp chopped fresh basil
2 tbsp tomato paste
salt and pepper

1 To make the meat sauce, heat the olive oil in a large skillet. Add the ground beef and cook, stirring frequently, until browned all over. Add the onion, celery, and garlic and cook for 3 minutes.

2 Sprinkle in the flour and cook, stirring constantly, for 1 minute. Gradually stir in the stock and red wine, season well with salt and pepper, and

add the parsley, marjoram, and basil. Bring to a boil, lower the heat, and simmer for 35 minutes. Add the tomato paste and simmer for 10 minutes longer.

3 Lightly grease an ovenproof dish with a little butter. Arrange sheets of lasagne over the base of the dish, spoon a layer of meat sauce over the noodles, then béchamel sauce. Place another layer

of lasagne on top and repeat the whole process twice, finishing with a layer of béchamel sauce. Lightly sprinkle with the grated mozzarella cheese.

4 Bake the lasagne in a preheated oven at 375°F for 35 minutes, until the top is golden brown and bubbling. Garnish with fresh basil, if desired, and serve immediately.

Pasticcio

Serves 6

INGREDIENTS

2 cups dried fusilli
1 tbsp olive oil, plus extra
   for brushing
4 tbsp heavy cream
salt
mixed salad, to serve

SAUCE:
2 tbsp olive oil
1 onion, thinly sliced

1 red bell pepper, cored,
   seeded, and chopped
2 garlic cloves, chopped
5^1/4 cups ground beef
14 ounce can chopped
   tomatoes
^{1}/2 cup dry white wine
2 tbsp chopped fresh parsley
2 ounce can anchovies,
   drained and chopped

salt and pepper

TOPPING:
1^1/4 cups natural yogurt
3 eggs
pinch of freshly grated
   nutmeg
^{1}/2 cup freshly grated
   Parmesan cheese

1 To make the sauce, heat the oil in a skillet and sauté the onion and red bell pepper for 3 minutes. Add the garlic and cook for 1 minute. Add the beef and cook until browned.

2 Add the tomatoes and wine and bring to a boil. Simmer for 20 minutes, until thickened.

Stir in the parsley, anchovies, and seasoning.

3 Bring a pan of salted water to a boil. Add the pasta and oil and cook for 10 minutes, until almost tender. Drain and transfer to a bowl. Stir in the cream.

4 For the topping, beat together the yogurt, eggs, and nutmeg.

5 Brush an ovenproof dish with oil. Spoon in half the pasta and cover with half the meat sauce. Repeat the process, then spread on the topping and sprinkle with cheese.

6 Bake in a preheated oven at 375°F for 25 minutes until golden. Serve with a mixed salad.

Fettuccine with Fillet of Veal & Pink Grapefruit in a Rose Petal Butter Sauce

Serves 4

INGREDIENTS

1 pound dried fettuccine
7 tbsp olive oil
1 tsp chopped fresh oregano
1 tsp chopped fresh marjoram
³/4 cup butter
1 pound veal fillet, thinly
   sliced
⁵/8 cup rose petal vinegar (see
   Cook's Tip)

⁵/8 cup fish stock
¹/4 cup grapefruit juice
¹/4 cup heavy cream
salt

TO GARNISH:

12 pink grapefruit segments
12 pink peppercorns
rose petals
fresh herb leaves

1 Cook the fettuccine with 1 tbsp of the oil in a pan of salted boiling water for 12 minutes. Drain and transfer to a warm serving dish. Add 2 tbsp of the olive oil, the oregano, and marjoram.

2 Heat 4 tbsp of the butter with the remaining oil in a large skillet. Gently fry the veal for 6 minutes. Remove and place on top of the pasta.

3 Add the vinegar and fish stock to the pan and bring to a boil. Boil vigorously until reduced by two-thirds. Add the grapefruit juice and cream and simmer for 4 minutes. Dice the remaining butter, add to the pan, and whisk until fully incorporated.

4 Pour the sauce around the veal, garnish and serve.

COOK'S TIP

To make rose petal vinegar, infuse the petals of 8 pesticide-free roses in ⁵/8 cup white wine vinegar for 48 hours.

Neapolitan Veal Cutlets with Mascarpone Cheese & Marille

Serves 4

INGREDIENTS

$^7/_8$ cup butter
4 9-ounce veal cutlets, trimmed
1 large onion, sliced
2 apples, peeled, cored, and sliced
6 ounces button mushrooms
1 tbsp chopped fresh tarragon

8 black peppercorns
1 tbsp sesame seeds
14 ounces dried marille
$^1/_2$ cup extra virgin olive oil
$^3/_4$ cup mascarpone cheese, broken into small pieces
salt and pepper

2 large beef tomatoes, cut in half
leaves of 1 fresh basil sprig
fresh basil leaves, to garnish

1 Melt 4 tbsp of the butter in a skillet and fry the veal for 5 minutes on each side. Transfer to a dish and keep warm.

2 Fry the onion and apples in the pan until lightly browned. Transfer to a dish, place the veal on top, and keep warm.

3 Fry the mushrooms, tarragon, and peppercorns in the remaining butter for 3 minutes. Sprinkle with the sesame seeds.

4 Bring a pan of salted water to a boil. Add the pasta and 1 tbsp of the oil and cook until tender. Drain and transfer to a serving plate.

5 Top the pasta with the mascarpone cheese and sprinkle with the remaining olive oil. Place the onions, apples and veal cutlets on top of the pasta. Spoon the mushrooms, peppercorns, and pan juices onto the cutlets, place the tomatoes and basil leaves around the edge, and place in a preheated oven at 300°F for 5 minutes. Season with salt and pepper to taste and serve immediately.

Stir-fried Pork with Pasta & Vegetables

Serves 4

INGREDIENTS

3 tbsp sesame oil
12 ounces pork tenderloin, cut into thin strips
1 pound dried taglioni
1 tbsp olive oil
8 shallots, sliced
2 garlic cloves, finely chopped
1-inch piece fresh ginger root, grated

1 fresh green chili, finely chopped
1 red bell pepper, cored, seeded, and thinly sliced
1 green bell pepper, cored, seeded, and thinly sliced
3 zucchini, thinly sliced
2 tbsp ground almonds
1 tsp ground cinnamon

1 tbsp oyster sauce
2 ounces creamed coconut (see Cook's Tip), grated
salt and pepper

1 Heat the sesame oil in a preheated wok. Season the pork and stir-fry for 5 minutes.

2 Bring a pan of salted water to a boil. Add the taglioni and olive oil and cook for 12 minutes. Set aside and keep warm.

3 Add the shallots, garlic, ginger, and chili to the wok and stir-fry for 2 minutes. Add the bell peppers and zucchini and stir-fry for 1 minute.

4 Finally, add the ground almonds, cinnamon, oyster sauce, and creamed coconut to the wok and stir-fry for 1 minute.

5 Drain the taglioni and transfer to a serving dish. Top with the stir-fry and serve immediately.

COOK'S TIP

Creamed coconut is available from Chinese and Asian food stores and some large supermarkets. It is sold in compressed blocks and adds a concentrated coconut flavor to the dish.

Orecchiette with Pork in Cream Sauce, garnished with Quail Eggs

Serves 4

INGREDIENTS

1 pound pork tenderloin, thinly sliced
4 tbsp olive oil
8 ounces button mushrooms, sliced

$^7/_8$ cup Italian red wine sauce (see page 52)
1 tbsp lemon juice
pinch of saffron
3 cups dried orecchiette
4 tbsp heavy cream

12 quail eggs (see Cook's Tip)
salt

1 Pound the slices of pork until wafer thin, then cut into strips.

2 Heat the olive oil in a skillet and stir-fry the pork for 5 minutes, then stir-fry the mushrooms for a further 2 minutes.

3 Pour in the Italian red wine sauce, then simmer for 20 minutes.

4 Meanwhile, bring a large saucepan of lightly salted water to a boil. Add the lemon juice, saffron, and orecchiette and cook for 12 minutes, until tender but still firm to the bite. Drain the pasta and keep warm.

5 Stir the cream into the pan with the pork and heat gently for 3 minutes.

6 Boil the quail eggs for 3 minutes, cool them in cold water, and remove the shells.

7 Transfer the pasta to a warm serving plate, top with the pork and sauce, and garnish with the eggs. Serve immediately.

COOK'S TIP

In this recipe, the quail eggs are soft-cooked. As they are very difficult to shell when warm, they should be thoroughly cooled first. Otherwise, they will break up unattractively.

Stuffed Cannelloni

Serves 4

INGREDIENTS

8 dried cannelloni tubes
1 tbsp olive oil
1/4 cup freshly grated
    Parmesan cheese
fresh herb sprigs, to garnish

FILLING:
2 tbsp butter
10 1/2 ounces frozen spinach,
    thawed and chopped

1/2 cup ricotta cheese
1/4 cup freshly grated
    Parmesan cheese
1/4 cup chopped ham
pinch of freshly grated
    nutmeg
2 tbsp heavy cream
2 eggs, lightly beaten
salt and pepper

SAUCE:
2 tbsp butter
1/4 cup all-purpose flour
1 1/4 cups milk
2 bay leaves
pinch of freshly grated
    nutmeg

1 For the filling, melt the butter in a pan and stir-fry the spinach for 2–3 minutes. Remove from the heat and stir in the cheeses and the ham. Season with nutmeg, salt, and pepper. Beat in the cream and eggs to make a thick paste.

2 Cook the pasta with the oil for 10–12 minutes, until almost tender. Drain and set aside.

3 To make the sauce, melt the butter in a pan. Stir in the flour and cook, stirring, for 1 minute. Gradually stir in the milk and the bay leaves and simmer for 5 minutes. Add the nutmeg and seasoning. Remove from the heat and discard the bay leaves.

4 Spoon the filling into a piping bag and fill the cannelloni.

5 Spoon a little sauce into the base of an ovenproof dish. Arrange the cannelloni in the dish in a single layer and pour over the remaining sauce. Sprinkle with the Parmesan cheese and bake in a preheated oven at 375°F for 40–45 minutes. Garnish with fresh herb sprigs and serve.

Tagliatelle with Pumpkin

Serves 4

INGREDIENTS

1 pound 2 ounces pumpkin or
   butternut squash, peeled
   and seeded
3 tbsp olive oil
1 onion, finely chopped
2 garlic cloves, crushed
4–6 tbsp chopped fresh
   parsley

pinch of freshly grated
   nutmeg
about 1¼ cups chicken or
   vegetable stock
4 ounces prosciutto
9 ounces dried tagliatelle
⅝ cup heavy cream
salt and pepper

freshly grated Parmesan
   cheese, to serve

1 Cut the pumpkin or butternut squash in half and scoop out the seeds. Cut the pumpkin or squash into ½-inch cubes.

2 Heat 2 tbsp of the oil in a large saucepan. Add the onion and garlic and fry over a low heat for about 3 minutes, until soft. Add half of the parsley and cook for 1 minute.

3 Add the pumpkin or squash pieces and cook for 2–3 minutes. Season to taste with salt, pepper, and nutmeg.

4 Add half of the stock to the pan, bring to a boil, cover, and simmer for 10 minutes, or until the pumpkin or squash is tender, adding more stock, if necessary.

5 Add the prosciutto to the pan and cook, stirring frequently for 2 minutes longer.

6 Bring a large pan of lightly salted water to a boil. Add the tagliatelle and the remaining oil and cook for 12 minutes, until tender, but still firm to the bite. Drain and transfer to a warm serving dish.

7 Stir the cream into the pumpkin and ham mixture and heat through. Spoon over the pasta, sprinkle with the remaining parsley, and serve with the Parmesan.

Eggplant Cake

Serves 4

INGREDIENTS

1 eggplant, thinly sliced
5 tbsp olive oil
2 cups dried fusilli
2¹/₂ cups Béchamel sauce (see page 166)
³/₄ cup grated cheddar cheese
butter, for greasing
¹/₃ cup freshly grated Parmesan cheese
salt and pepper

LAMB SAUCE:
2 tbsp olive oil
1 large onion, sliced
2 celery stalks, thinly sliced
1 pound ground lamb
3 tbsp tomato paste
5¹/₂ ounces bottled sun-dried tomatoes, drained and chopped
1 tsp dried oregano

1 tbsp red wine vinegar
⁵/₈ cup chicken stock
salt and pepper

1 Sprinkle the eggplant slices with salt and set aside for 45 minutes.

2 To make the sauce, fry the onion and celery in the oil for 3–4 minutes. Add the lamb and cook until browned. Stir in the remaining sauce ingredients and cook for 20 minutes.

3 Rinse the eggplant slices, drain, and pat dry. Heat 4 tbsp of the oil in a skillet. Fry the eggplant slices for about 4 minutes on each side. Remove from the skillet and drain well.

4 Cook the fusilli with the oil in a pan of salted boiling water, until tender, but still firm to the bite. Drain and keep warm.

5 Gently heat the béchamel sauce. Stir in the cheddar cheese and then stir half of the cheese sauce into the fusilli.

6 Make layers of fusilli, lamb sauce, and eggplant slices in a greased dish. Spread the remaining cheese sauce over the top. Sprinkle with the Parmesan and bake in a preheated oven at 375°F for 25 minutes. Serve hot or cold.

Whole-wheat Spaghetti with Suprêmes of Chicken Nell Gwyn

Serves 4

INGREDIENTS

1/8 cup rapeseed oil

3 tbsp olive oil

4 8-ounce chicken suprêmes

5/8 cup orange brandy

2 tbsp all-purpose flour

5/8 cup freshly squeezed orange juice

1 ounce zucchini, cut into matchstick strips

1 ounce red bell pepper, cut into matchstick strips

1 ounce leek, finely shredded

14 ounces dried whole-wheat spaghetti

3 large oranges, peeled and cut into segments

rind of 1 orange, cut into very fine strips

2 tbsp chopped fresh tarragon

5/8 cup fromage frais or ricotta cheese

salt and pepper

1 Heat the rapeseed oil and 1 tbsp of the olive oil in a skillet. Add the chicken and cook quickly until golden brown. Add the orange brandy and cook for 3 minutes. Add the flour and cook for 2 minutes.

2 Lower the heat and add the orange juice, zucchini, bell pepper, and leek, and season. Simmer for 5 minutes until the sauce has thickened.

3 Meanwhile, bring a pan of salted water to a boil. Add the spaghetti and 1 tbsp of the olive oil and cook for 10 minutes, until just tender, but still firm to the bite. Drain, transfer to a serving dish, and drizzle the remaining oil on top.

4 Add half the orange segments, half the orange rind, the tarragon, and fromage frais or ricotta cheese to the sauce in the pan and cook for 3 minutes.

5 Place the chicken on top of the pasta, pour over a little sauce, garnish with orange segments and rind. Serve immediately.

Chicken & Mushroom Lasagne

Serves 4

INGREDIENTS

butter, for greasing
14 sheets precooked lasagne
3³/₄ cups béchamel sauce (see page 166)
1 cup grated Parmesan cheese

CHICKEN & MUSHROOM SAUCE:
2 tbsp olive oil
2 garlic cloves, crushed
1 large onion, finely chopped
8 ounces exotic mushrooms, sliced
2¹/₂ cups ground chicken
3 ounces chicken livers, finely chopped

4 ounces prosciutto, diced
⁵/₈ cup Marsala
10 ounce can chopped tomatoes
1 tbsp chopped fresh basil leaves
2 tbsp tomato paste
salt and pepper

1 To make the sauce, heat the olive oil in a large pan. Add the garlic, onion, and mushrooms and cook, stirring frequently, for 6 minutes.

2 Add the ground chicken, chicken livers, and prosciutto and cook over a low heat for 12 minutes, until the meat has browned.

3 Stir the Marsala, tomatoes, basil, and tomato paste into the pan and cook for 4 minutes. Season to taste, cover, and simmer for 30 minutes. Uncover the pan, stir, and simmer for an additional 15 minutes.

4 Arrange sheets of lasagne over the base of a greased ovenproof dish, spoon a layer of chicken and mushroom sauce over the lasagne, then add a layer of béchamel sauce. Place another layer of lasagne on top and repeat the process twice, finishing with a layer of béchamel sauce. Sprinkle with the grated cheese and bake in a preheated oven at 375°F for 35 minutes until golden brown. Serve.

Tagliatelle with Chicken Sauce

Serves 4

INGREDIENTS

9 ounces fresh green
   tagliatelle
1 tbsp olive oil
salt
fresh basil leaves, to garnish

TOMATO SAUCE:
2 tbsp olive oil
1 small onion, chopped
1 garlic clove, chopped

14 ounce can chopped
   tomatoes
2 tbsp chopped fresh parsley
1 tsp dried oregano
2 bay leaves
2 tbsp tomato paste
1 tsp sugar
salt and pepper

CHICKEN SAUCE:
4 tbsp unsalted butter
14 ounces boned chicken
   breasts, skinned, and cut
   into thin strips
$^3/_4$ cup blanched almonds
$1^1/_4$ cups heavy cream
salt and pepper

1 To make the tomato sauce, heat the oil in a pan and fry the onion until translucent. Add the garlic and cook for 1 minute. Stir in the tomatoes, parsley, oregano, bay leaves, tomato paste, and sugar. Season, bring to a boil, and simmer for 15–20 minutes, until reduced by half. Remove from the heat and discard the bay leaves.

2 To make the chicken sauce, melt the butter in a skillet and stir-fry the chicken and almonds for 5–6 minutes, until the chicken is cooked through.

3 Meanwhile, bring the cream to a boil in a pan and boil for about 10 minutes, until reduced by half. Pour the cream over the chicken and almonds,

stir, and season to taste. Set aside and keep warm.

4 Bring a large pan of salted water to a boil. Add the tagliatelle and olive oil and cook until tender. Drain and transfer to a warm serving dish. Spoon the tomato sauce over the pasta and arrange the chicken sauce on top. Garnish and serve.

Mustard Baked Chicken with Pasta Shells

Serves 4

INGREDIENTS

8 chicken pieces
  (about 4 ounces each)
4 tbsp butter, melted
4 tbsp mild mustard (see
  Cook's Tip)

2 tbsp lemon juice
1 tbsp brown sugar
1 tsp paprika
3 tbsp poppy seeds
14 ounces fresh pasta shells

1 tbsp olive oil
salt and pepper

1 Arrange the chicken, smooth side down, in an ovenproof dish.

2 Mix together the butter, mustard, lemon juice, sugar, and paprika in a bowl and season to taste. Brush the mixture over the upper surfaces of the chicken pieces and bake in a preheated oven at 400°F for 15 minutes.

3 Remove the dish from the oven and carefully turn over the chicken pieces. Coat the upper surfaces of the chicken with the remaining mustard mixture, sprinkle with poppy seeds, and return to the oven for 15 minutes longer.

4 Meanwhile, bring a large pan of lightly salted water to a boil. Add the pasta shells and olive oil and cook until tender, but still firm to the bite.

5 Drain the pasta and arrange on a warmed serving dish. Top with the chicken, pour over the sauce, and serve immediately.

COOK'S TIP

Dijon is the type of mustard most often used in cooking, as it has a clean and only mildly spicy flavor. German mustard has a sweet-sour taste, with Bavarian mustard being slightly sweeter. American mustard is mild and sweet.

Tortellini

Serves 4

INGREDIENTS

4 ounces boned chicken
  breast, skinned
2 ounces prosciutto
1½ ounces cooked spinach,
  well drained
1 tbsp finely chopped onion
2 tbsp freshly grated
  Parmesan cheese
pinch of ground allspice

1 egg, beaten
1 pound Basic Pasta Dough
  (see page 4)
salt and pepper
2 tbsp chopped fresh parsley,
  to garnish

SAUCE:
1¼ cups light cream
2 garlic cloves, crushed
4 ounces button mushrooms,
  thinly sliced
4 tbsp freshly grated
  Parmesan cheese

1 Bring a pan of seasoned water to a boil. Add the chicken and poach for 10 minutes. Cool slightly, then put in a food processor with the prosciutto, spinach, and onion, and process until finely chopped. Stir in the Parmesan cheese, allspice, and egg and season to taste.

2 Thinly roll out the pasta dough and cut into 1½–2-inch rounds.

3 Place ½ tsp of the filling in the center of each round. Fold the pieces in half and press the edges to seal. Then wrap each piece around your index finger, cross over the ends, and curl the rest of the dough backward to make a navel shape.

4 Bring a pan of salted water to a boil. Add the tortellini, in batches, bring back to a boil, and cook for

5 minutes. Drain and transfer to a serving dish.

5 To make the sauce, bring the cream and garlic to a boil in a pan, then simmer for 3 minutes. Add the mushrooms and half the cheese, season, and simmer for 2–3 minutes. Pour the sauce over the pasta. Sprinkle with the remaining Parmesan, garnish and serve.

Chicken Suprêmes Filled with Tiger Shrimp on a Bed of Pasta

Serves 4

INGREDIENTS

4 7-ounce chicken
  suprêmes, trimmed
4 ounces large spinach leaves,
  trimmed and blanched in
  hot salted water
4 slices of prosciutto

12–16 raw tiger shrimp,
  shelled and deveined
4 tbsp butter, plus extra
  for greasing
1 pound dried tagliatelle
1 tbsp olive oil

3 leeks, shredded
1 large carrot, grated
$5/8$ cup thick mayonnaise
2 large cooked beets
salt

1 Place each suprême between 2 pieces of waxed paper and pound with a rolling pin to flatten.

2 Divide half of the spinach among the suprêmes, add a slice of prosciutto to each, and top with more spinach. Place 4 shrimp on top. Roll up each suprême to form a packet. Wrap each packet in greased foil, place on a cookie sheet and bake in a preheated oven at 400°F for 20 minutes.

3 Cook the pasta with the oil in salted boiling water, until tender. Drain and transfer to a warm dish.

4 Melt the butter and fry the leeks and carrot for 3 minutes. Transfer to the center of the pasta.

5 Work the mayonnaise and 1 beet in a food processor or blender until smooth. Rub through a strainer and pour around the pasta and vegetables.

6 Cut the remaining beet into diamond shapes and place them neatly around the mayonnaise. Remove the foil from the chicken and cut the suprêmes into thin slices. Arrange the slices on top of the vegetables and pasta, and serve.

Chicken & Lobster on a Bed of Penne

Serves 6

INGREDIENTS

butter, for greasing	salt	2 shallots, very finely chopped
6 chicken breasts	lemon wedges, to serve	2 figs, chopped
1 pound dried penne rigate		1 tbsp Marsala
6 tbsp extra virgin olive oil	FILLING:	2 tbsp breadcrumbs
1 cup freshly grated	4 ounces lobster meat,	1 large egg, beaten
Parmesan cheese	chopped	salt and pepper

1 Grease 6 pieces of foil large enough to enclose each chicken breast and lightly grease a cookie sheet.

2 Place all of the filling ingredients into a mixing bowl and blend together thoroughly with a spoon.

3 Cut a pocket in each chicken breast with a sharp knife and fill with the lobster mixture. Wrap each chicken breast in foil, place the packets on the greased cookie sheet, and bake in a preheated oven at 400°F for 30 minutes.

4 Meanwhile, bring a large pan of lightly salted water to a boil. Add the pasta and 1 tablespoon of the olive oil and cook for about 10 minutes, or until tender but still firm to the bite. Drain the pasta thoroughly and transfer to a large serving plate. Sprinkle with the remaining olive oil and the grated Parmesan cheese, set aside, and keep warm until required.

5 Carefully remove the foil from around the chicken breasts. Slice the breasts very thinly and arrange over the pasta. Serve with lemon wedges.

COOK'S TIP

The cut of chicken known as suprême consists of the breast and wing. It is always skinned.

Chicken with Green Olives & Pasta

Serves 4

INGREDIENTS

3 tbsp olive oil

2 tbsp butter

4 chicken breasts, part boned

1 large onion, finely chopped

2 garlic cloves, crushed

2 red, yellow, or green bell
   peppers, cored, seeded, and
   cut into large pieces

9 ounces button mushrooms,
   sliced or quartered

6 ounces tomatoes, skinned
   and halved

$5/8$ cup dry white wine

$1^1/2$ cups pitted green olives

4–6 tbsp heavy cream

14 ounces dried pasta

salt and pepper

chopped parsley, to garnish

1 Heat 2 tbsp of the oil and the butter in a skillet. Fry the chicken breasts until golden brown. Remove from the pan.

2 Add the onion and garlic to the pan and sauté over a medium heat until beginning to soften. Add the bell peppers and mushrooms and cook for 2–3 minutes. Add the tomatoes and season to taste with salt and pepper. Transfer the vegetables to a casserole and arrange the chicken on top.

3 Add the wine to the pan and bring to a boil. Pour the wine over the chicken. Cover and cook in a preheated oven at 350°F for 50 minutes.

4 Add the olives to the casserole and mix in until well combined. Pour in the cream, cover, and return to the oven for 10–20 minutes.

5 Bring a large pan of lightly salted water to a boil. Add the pasta and the remaining oil and cook until tender, but still firm to the bite. Drain well and transfer to a serving dish.

6 Arrange the chicken on top of the pasta, cover with the sauce, garnish with the parsley, and serve immediately. Alternatively, place the pasta in a large serving bowl and serve separately.

Sliced Breast of Duckling with Linguine

Serves 4

INGREDIENTS

4 $10^1/_2$-ounce boned breasts
  of duckling
2 tbsp butter
$3/_8$ cup finely chopped carrots
4 tbsp finely chopped shallots
1 tbsp lemon juice
$5/_8$ cup meat stock
4 tbsp clear honey

$3/_4$ cup fresh or thawed
  frozen raspberries
$1/_4$ cup all-purpose flour
1 tbsp Worcestershire sauce
14 ounces fresh linguine
1 tbsp olive oil
salt and pepper

TO GARNISH:
fresh raspberries
fresh sprigs of parsley

1 Trim and score the duck breasts and season well. Melt the butter in a skillet and fry the duck breasts until lightly colored.

2 Add the carrots, shallots, lemon juice, and half the meat stock and simmer for 1 minute. Stir in half the honey and half the raspberries. Sprinkle in half the flour and cook, stirring constantly, for 3 minutes. Add pepper and the Worcestershire sauce.

3 Stir in the remaining stock and cook for 1 minute. Stir in the remaining honey, raspberries, and flour. Cook for 3 minutes longer.

4 Remove the duck from the pan, but continue simmering the sauce.

5 Bring a large pan of salted water to a boil. Add the linguine and olive oil and cook until tender. Drain and divide between 4 individual plates.

6 Slice the duck breasts lengthwise into $1/_4$-inch thick pieces. Pour a little sauce over the pasta and arrange the sliced duck in a fan shape on top of it. Garnish and serve.

Rigatoni & Pesto Baked Partridge

Serves 4

INGREDIENTS

8 partridge pieces
(about 4 ounces each)
4 tbsp butter, melted
4 tbsp Dijon mustard
2 tbsp lime juice

1 tbsp brown sugar
6 tbsp pesto sauce
(see page 12)
1 pound dried rigatoni
1 tbsp olive oil

1 1/3 cups freshly grated
Parmesan cheese
salt and pepper

1 Arrange the partridge pieces, smooth side down, in a single layer in a large, ovenproof dish.

2 Mix together the butter, Dijon mustard, lime juice, and brown sugar in a bowl. Season to taste with salt and pepper. Brush this mixture over the uppermost surfaces of the partridge pieces and bake in a preheated oven at 400°F for 15 minutes.

3 Remove the dish from the oven and coat the partridge pieces with 3 tbsp of the pesto sauce. Return to the oven and bake for a further 12 minutes.

4 Remove the dish from the oven and carefully turn over the partridge pieces. Coat the top of the partridges with the remaining mustard mixture and return to the oven for a further 10 minutes.

5 Meanwhile, bring a large pan of lightly salted water to a boil. Add the rigatoni and olive oil and cook for about 10 minutes, until tender, but still firm to the bite. Drain and transfer to a large serving dish. Toss the pasta with the remaining pesto sauce and the Parmesan.

6 Arrange the pieces of partridge on the serving dish with the rigatoni, pour the cooking juices on top, and serve immediately.

VARIATION

You could also prepare young pheasant in the same way.

Breast of Pheasant Lasagne with Baby Onions & Green Peas

Serves 4

INGREDIENTS

butter, for greasing
14 sheets precooked lasagne
3³/₄ cups Béchamel sauce (see page 166)
³/₄ cup grated mozzarella cheese

FILLING:
8 ounces pork fat, diced
2 tbsp butter
16 small onions
8 large pheasant breasts, thinly sliced
¹/₄ cup all-purpose flour

2¹/₂ cups chicken stock
bouquet garni
1 pound fresh peas, shelled
salt and pepper

1 Put the pork fat into a pan of boiling, salted water. Simmer for 3 minutes, drain and pat dry.

2 Fry the pork fat and onions in the butter until lightly browned. Remove from the pan.

3 Add the pheasant to the pan and cook over a low heat, until browned all over. Transfer to an ovenproof dish.

4 Stir the flour into the pan and cook until just brown, then blend in the stock. Pour over the pheasant, add the bouquet garni, and cook in a preheated oven at 400°F for 5 minutes.

5 Remove and discard the bouquet garni. Add the onions, pork fat, and peas and return to the oven for about 10 minutes.

6 Mince the pheasant breasts and pork in a food processor.

7 Lower the oven to 375°F. Make layers of lasagne, pheasant sauce, and béchamel sauce in a greased ovenproof dish, ending with béchamel sauce. Sprinkle with the cheese and bake in the oven for 30 minutes. Serve surrounded by the peas and onions.

Fish & Seafood

Pasta is a natural partner for fish
and seafood. Both are cooked quickly to
preserve their flavor and texture, they are
packed full of nutritional goodness, and the
varieties available are almost infinite. The
superb recipes in this chapter demonstrate the
full range of these qualities. For a quick,
easy, and satisfying supper, try Spaghetti al
Tonno, Casserole of Fusilli & Smoked
Haddock with Egg Sauce, Seafood Lasagne,
or Macaroni and Shrimp Bake. More unusual
and sophisticated dishes include Sea Bass with
Olive Sauce on a Bed of Macaroni, Poached
Salmon Steaks with Penne, Farfallini Buttered
Lobster, and Baked Scallops with Pasta
in Shells. There are dishes to suit all
tastes—freshwater and sea fish, shellfish and
other seafood—and to suit all pockets.
All are easy to make; the only problem
is choosing which one to cook next.

Cannelloni Filetti di Sogliola

Serves 6

INGREDIENTS

12 small fillets of sole
(about 4 ounces each)
$5/8$ cup red wine
6 tbsp butter
$3^7/8$ cups sliced
button mushrooms
4 shallots, finely chopped

4 ounces tomatoes, chopped
2 tbsp tomato paste
$1/2$ cup all-purpose
flour, sifted
$5/8$ cup warm milk
2 tbsp heavy cream
6 dried cannelloni tubes

6 ounces cooked, peeled
shrimp, preferably
freshwater
salt and pepper
1 fresh fennel sprig, to garnish

1 Brush the fillets with a little wine, season, then roll them up, skin side inward. Secure with a skewer or toothpick.

2 Arrange the fish rolls in a single layer in a large skillet, add the remaining red wine, and poach for about 4 minutes. Remove the fish, reserving the cooking liquid.

3 Melt the butter in another pan. Sauté the mushrooms and shallots

for 2 minutes, then add the tomatoes and tomato paste. Season the flour and stir it into the pan. Stir in the reserved cooking liquid and half the milk. Cook over a low heat, stirring, for 4 minutes. Remove from the heat and stir in the cream.

4 Bring a pan of salted water to a boil. Add the cannelloni and cook for 8 minutes, until tender but still firm to the bite. Drain and set aside to cool.

5 Remove the skewers or toothpicks from the fish rolls. Put 2 sole fillets into each cannelloni tube with 2–3 shrimp and a little red wine sauce. Arrange the cannelloni in an ovenproof dish, pour over the sauce and bake in a preheated oven at 400°F for 20 minutes.

6 Transfer the cannelloni to individual serving plates, garnish, and serve with the red wine sauce.

Sea Bass with Olive Sauce on a Bed of Macaroni

Serves 4

INGREDIENTS

1 pound dried macaroni
1 tbsp olive oil
8 4-ounce sea bass medallions

TO GARNISH:
lemon slices
shredded leek
shredded carrot

SAUCE:
2 tbsp butter
4 shallots, chopped
2 tbsp capers
1 1/2 cups pitted green olives,
   chopped
4 tbsp balsamic vinegar
1 1/4 cups fish stock
1 1/4 cups heavy cream

juice of 1 lemon
salt and pepper

---

1 To make the sauce, melt the butter in a skillet and fry the shallots for 4 minutes. Add the capers and olives and cook for 3 minutes longer.

2 Stir in the balsamic vinegar and fish stock, bring to a boil, and reduce by half. Add the cream, stirring, and reduce again by half. Season to taste and

stir in the lemon juice. Remove from the heat, set aside, and keep warm.

3 Bring a pan of salted water to a boil. Add the pasta and olive oil and cook for 12 minutes, until tender but still firm to the bite.

4 Meanwhile, lightly broil the sea bass medallions for 3–4 minutes

on each side, until cooked through, but still moist and delicate.

5 Drain the pasta and transfer to a large serving dish. Top the pasta with the fish medallions and then pour on the olive sauce. Garnish with a few lemon slices, shredded leek, and shredded carrot and serve immediately.

Spaghetti alla Bucaniera

Serves 4

INGREDIENTS

3/4 cup all-purpose flour
1 pound brill or sole fillets, skinned and chopped
1 pound hake fillets, skinned and chopped
6 tbsp butter
4 shallots, finely chopped
2 garlic cloves, crushed

1 carrot, diced
1 leek, finely chopped
1 1/4 cups hard cider
1 1/4 cups medium sweet cider
2 tsp anchovy extract
1 tbsp tarragon vinegar
1 pound dried spaghetti
1 tbsp olive oil

salt and pepper
chopped fresh parsley, to garnish
crusty brown bread, to serve

1 Season the flour with salt and pepper to taste. Sprinkle 1/4 cup of the seasoned flour onto a shallow plate. Press the fish pieces into the seasoned flour so that they are thoroughly coated.

2 Melt the butter in a flameproof casserole. Add the fish fillets, shallots, garlic, carrot, and leek and cook over a low heat, stirring frequently, for about 10 minutes.

3 Sprinkle over the remaining seasoned flour and cook, stirring constantly, for 2 minutes. Gradually stir in the cider, anchovy extract, and tarragon vinegar. Bring to a boil and simmer over a low heat for 35 minutes. Alternatively, bake in a preheated oven at 350°F for 30 minutes.

4 About 15 minutes before the end of the cooking time, bring a large

pan of lightly salted water to a boil. Add the spaghetti and olive oil and cook for about 12 minutes, until tender but still firm to the bite. Drain the spaghetti thoroughly and transfer to a large serving dish.

5 Arrange the fish on top of the spaghetti and cover with the sauce. Garnish with chopped parsley and serve immediately with warm, crusty brown bread.

Steamed Pasta Pudding

Serves 4

INGREDIENTS

1 cup dried short-cut macaroni or other short pasta	2–3 fresh parsley sprigs	$^2/_3$ cup freshly grated Parmesan cheese
1 tbsp olive oil	6 black peppercorns	salt and pepper
1 tbsp butter, plus extra for greasing	$^1/_2$ cup heavy cream	fresh dill or parsley sprigs, to garnish
1 pound white fish fillets, such as cod or haddock	2 eggs, separated	tomato sauce (see page 54), to serve
	2 tbsp chopped fresh dill or parsley	
	pinch of freshly grated nutmeg	

1 Bring a pan of salted water to a boil. Add the pasta and olive oil and cook until tender, but still firm to the bite. Drain the pasta, add the butter, cover, and keep warm.

2 Place the fish in a skillet. Add the parsley sprigs, peppercorns, and enough water to cover. Bring to a boil, cover, and simmer for 10 minutes. Remove the fish, reserving the cooking liquid.

3 Skin the fish and cut into bite-size pieces. Combine the cream, egg yolks, chopped dill or parsley, nutmeg, and cheese, and mix with the pasta in a bowl. Spoon in the fish and enough of the reserved cooking liquid to make a moist, but firm mixture. Whisk the egg whites until stiff, then fold them into the mixture.

4 Grease a heatproof bowl and spoon in the fish mixture to within 1½ inches of the rim. Cover the top with greased baking paper and foil and tie securely with a piece of string.

5 Stand the bowl on a trivet in a saucepan. Add boiling water to reach halfway up the sides. Cover and steam for 1½ hours. Invert the pudding onto a serving plate. Garnish and serve with the tomato sauce.

Red Mullet Fillets with Orecchiette, Amaretto, & Orange Sauce

Serves 4

INGREDIENTS

³/4 cup all-purpose flour
8 red mullet fillets
2 tbsp butter
⁵/8 cup fish stock
1 tbsp crushed almonds
1 tsp pink peppercorns
1 orange, peeled and cut
  into segments

1 tbsp orange liqueur
grated rind of 1 orange
1 pound dried orecchiette
1 tbsp olive oil
⁵/8 cup heavy cream
4 tbsp amaretto
salt and pepper

TO GARNISH:
2 tbsp snipped fresh chives
1 tbsp toasted almonds

1 Season the flour and sprinkle into a shallow bowl. Press the fish fillets into the flour to coat. Melt the butter in a skillet and fry the fish over a low heat for 3 minutes, until browned.

2 Add the fish stock to the pan and cook for 4 minutes. Carefully remove the fish, cover with foil, and keep warm.

3 Add the almonds, pink peppercorns, half the orange, the orange liqueur, and orange rind to the pan. Simmer until the liquid has reduced by half.

4 Meanwhile, bring a large saucepan of lightly salted water to a boil. Add the orecchiette and olive oil and cook for 15 minutes, until tender but still firm to the bite.

5 Meanwhile, season the sauce and stir in the cream and amaretto. Cook for 2 minutes. Return the fish to the pan to coat with the sauce.

6 Drain the pasta and transfer to a serving dish. Top with the fish fillets and their sauce. Garnish with orange segments, chives, and toasted almonds. Serve.

Vermicelli with Fillets of Red Mullet

Serves 4

INGREDIENTS

2¹/₄ pounds red mullet fillets
1¹/₄ cups dry white wine
4 shallots, finely chopped
1 garlic clove, crushed
3 tbsp mixed fresh herbs
finely grated rind and juice of
    1 lemon

pinch of freshly grated
    nutmeg
3 anchovy fillets, roughly
    chopped
2 tbsp heavy cream
1 tsp cornstarch
1 pound dried vermicelli

1 tbsp olive oil
salt and pepper

TO GARNISH:
1 fresh mint sprig
lemon slices
lemon rind

1 Put the fish fillets in a large casserole. Pour the wine over and add the shallots, garlic, chopped herbs, lemon rind and juice, nutmeg, and anchovies. Season to taste. Cover and bake in a preheated oven at 350°F for 35 minutes.

2 Carefully transfer the mullet to a warm dish. Set aside and keep warm while you prepare the sauce and pasta.

3 Pour the cooking liquid into a pan and bring to a boil. Simmer for 25 minutes, until reduced by half. Mix together the cream and cornstarch and stir into the sauce to thicken.

4 Bring a pan of salted water to a boil. Add the vermicelli and olive oil and cook until tender, but still firm to the bite. Drain the pasta and transfer to a warm serving dish.

5 Arrange the red mullet fillets on top of the vermicelli and pour the sauce over it. Garnish with a fresh mint sprig, slices of lemon, and strips of lemon rind and serve immediately.

COOK'S TIP

The best red mullet is sometimes called golden mullet, although it is bright red in color.

Spaghetti al Tonno

Serves 4

INGREDIENTS

7 ounce can tuna, drained

2 ounce can anchovies, drained

1 1/8 cups olive oil

1 cup roughly chopped parsley

5/8 cup crème fraîche

1 pound dried spaghetti

2 tbsp butter

salt and pepper

black olives, to garnish

crusty bread, to serve

1 Remove any bones from the tuna. Put the tuna into a food processor or blender, together with the anchovies, 1 cup of the olive oil, and the parsley. Process until smooth.

2 Spoon the crème fraîche into the food processor or blender and process again for a few seconds to blend thoroughly. Season to taste.

3 Bring a large pan of lightly salted water to a boil. Add the spaghetti and the remaining olive oil and cook until tender, but still firm to the bite.

4 Drain the spaghetti, return to the saucepan and place over a medium heat. Add the butter and toss well to coat. Spoon in the sauce and quickly toss into the spaghetti, using 2 forks, until well combined.

5 Remove the pan from the heat and divide the spaghetti between 4 warm individual plates. Garnish with the olives and serve immediately with warm, crusty bread.

VARIATION

If desired, you could add 1–2 garlic cloves to the sauce, substitute 1/2 cup chopped fresh basil for half the parsley, and garnish with capers instead of black olives.

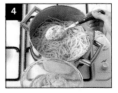

Casserole of Fusilli & Smoked Haddock with Egg Sauce

Serves 4

INGREDIENTS

2 tbsp butter, plus extra
    for greasing
1 pound smoked haddock
    fillets, cut into 4 slices
2¹/₂ cups milk
¹/₄ cup all-purpose flour

pinch of freshly grated
    nutmeg
3 tbsp heavy cream
1 tbsp chopped fresh parsley,
    plus extra to garnish

2 eggs, hard cooked and
    mashed to a pulp
4 cups dried fusilli
1 tbsp lemon juice
salt and pepper
boiled new potatoes and
    beets, to serve

1 Grease a casserole with butter. Put the haddock in the casserole and pour in the milk. Bake in a preheated oven at 400°F for 15 minutes. Carefully pour the cooking liquid into a pitcher without breaking up the fish.

2 Melt the butter in a saucepan and stir in the flour. Gradually whisk in the reserved cooking liquid. Season with salt, pepper, and nutmeg. Stir in the cream, parsley, and mashed egg and cook for 2 minutes.

3 Bring a large saucepan of lightly salted water to a boil. Add the fusilli and lemon juice and cook until tender, but still firm to the bite.

4 Drain the pasta and tip it over the fish. Top with the sauce and return to the oven for 10 minutes.

5 Garnish and serve the casserole with boiled new potatoes and beets.

VARIATION

You can use any type of dried pasta for this casserole. Try penne, conchiglie, or rigatoni.

Ravioli of Lemon Sole & Haddock

Serves 4

INGREDIENTS

1 pound lemon sole fillets, skinned
1 pound haddock fillets, skinned
3 eggs beaten
1 pound cooked potato gnocchi (see page 58)

3 cups fresh breadcrumbs
1/4 cup heavy cream
1 pound Basic Pasta Dough (see page 4)
1 1/4 cups Italian red wine sauce (see page 52)

2/3 cup freshly grated Parmesan cheese
salt and pepper

---

1 Flake the fish fillets in a large mixing bowl.

2 Mix the eggs, cooked potato gnocchi, breadcrumbs, and cream in a bowl until combined. Add the fish to the bowl and season to taste.

3 Roll out the pasta dough on a lightly floured counter and cut out 3-inch rounds.

4 Place a spoonful of the fish stuffing on each round. Dampen the edges slightly and fold the pasta rounds over, pressing together to seal.

5 Bring a large saucepan of lightly salted water to a boil. Add the ravioli and cook for 15 minutes.

6 Transfer the ravioli, using a slotted spoon, to a large serving dish. Pour the Italian red wine sauce over the ravioli, sprinkle with the Parmesan cheese, and serve immediately.

COOK'S TIP

For square ravioli, divide the dough into two. Wrap half in plastic wrap and thinly roll out the other half. Cover with a clean, damp dish cloth while you roll the remaining dough. Spoon the filling at regular intervals brushing the gaps with water or beaten egg. Cover with the second sheet of dough and press firmly between the filling to seal and expel any air. Cut into squares.

Poached Salmon Steaks with Penne

Serves 4

INGREDIENTS

4 10-ounce fresh salmon
  steaks
4 tbsp butter
$^3/_4$ cup dry white wine
sea salt
8 peppercorns
fresh dill sprig
fresh tarragon sprig
1 lemon, sliced

1 pound dried penne
2 tbsp olive oil
lemon slices and fresh
  watercress, to garnish

LEMON & WATERCRESS
  SAUCE:
2 tbsp butter
$^1/_4$ cup all-purpose flour

$^5/_8$ cup warm milk
juice and finely grated rind of
  2 lemons
2 ounces watercress, chopped
salt and pepper

1 Put the salmon in a large, nonstick pan. Add the butter, wine, a pinch of sea salt, the peppercorns, dill, tarragon, and lemon. Cover, bring to a boil, and simmer for 10 minutes.

2 Using a fish slice, remove the salmon. Strain and reserve the cooking liquid. Remove and discard the salmon skin and center bones.

Place the fish on a warm dish, cover, and keep warm.

3 Bring a saucepan of salted water to a boil. Add the penne and 1 tbsp of the oil and cook for 12 minutes. Drain and toss in the remaining olive oil. Place on a warm serving dish, top with the salmon steaks, and keep warm.

4 To make the sauce, melt the butter and stir

in the flour for 2 minutes. Stir in the milk and about 7 tbsp of the reserved cooking liquid. Add the lemon juice and rind and cook, stirring, for 10 minutes.

5 Add the watercress to the sauce, stir gently, and season to taste.

6 Pour the sauce over the salmon and penne, garnish, and serve.

Spaghetti with Smoked Salmon

Serves 4

INGREDIENTS

1 pound dried buckwheat
   spaghetti
2 tbsp olive oil
$^1/_2$ cup crumbled feta cheese
salt
fresh cilantro or parsley
   leaves, to garnish

SAUCE:
$1^1/_4$ cups heavy cream
$^5/_8$ cup whiskey or brandy
$4^1/_2$ ounces smoked salmon
pinch of cayenne pepper
black pepper

2 tbsp chopped fresh cilantro
   or parsley

1 Bring a large pan of lightly salted water to a boil. Add the spaghetti and 1 tbsp of the olive oil and cook until tender, but still firm to the bite. Drain and toss in the remaining olive oil. Cover, shake the pan, set aside, and keep warm.

2 Pour the cream into a small saucepan and bring to simmering point, but do not let it boil. Pour the whiskey or brandy into another small saucepan and bring to simmering point, but do not allow it to boil. Remove both pans from the heat and mix together the cream and whiskey or brandy.

3 Cut the smoked salmon into thin strips and add to the cream mixture. Season to taste with cayenne and black pepper. Just before serving, add the chopped fresh cilantro or parsley and stir until well combined.

4 Transfer the spaghetti to a warm serving dish, pour the sauce on, and toss thoroughly with 2 large forks. Scatter the crumbled feta cheese over the top, garnish with the cilantro or parsley leaves, and serve immediately.

COOK'S TIP

Serve this rich and luxurious dish with a green salad tossed in a lemony dressing.

Trout with Pasta Colle Acciughe & Smoked Bacon

Serves 4

INGREDIENTS

butter, for greasing
4 9$^{1}/_{2}$-ounce trout, gutted
   and cleaned
12 anchovies in oil, drained
   and chopped
2 apples, peeled, cored, and
   sliced

4 fresh mint sprigs
juice of 1 lemon
12 slices bacon
1 pound dried tagliatelle
1 tbsp olive oil
salt and pepper

TO GARNISH:
2 apples, cored and sliced
4 fresh mint sprigs

1 Open up the cavities of each trout and wash with warm salt water.

2 Season each cavity with salt and black pepper. Divide the anchovies, sliced apples, and mint sprigs between each of the cavities. Sprinkle the lemon juice into each cavity.

3 Carefully wrap each trout with three slices of bacon in a spiral, covering all of the fish except for the head and tail.

4 Arrange the trout on a deep, greased cookie sheet with the loose ends of bacon tucked neatly underneath. Season with black pepper to taste and bake in a preheated oven at 400°F for 20 minutes, turning the trout over after 10 minutes.

5 Meanwhile, bring a large pan of lightly salted water to a boil. Add the tagliatelle and olive oil and cook for 12 minutes, until tender, but still firm to the bite. Drain and transfer to a serving dish.

6 Remove the trout from the oven and arrange on the tagliatelle. Garnish with sliced apples and fresh mint sprigs and serve immediately.

Farfalle with a Medley of Seafood

Serves 4

INGREDIENTS

12 raw tiger shrimp
12 raw shrimp
4¹/₂ ounces freshwater shrimp
1 pound fillet of sea bream
4 tbsp butter
12 scallops, shelled
juice and finely grated rind of
    1 lemon

pinch of saffron powder or
    threads
4 cups vegetable stock
⁵/₈ cup rose petal vinegar (see
    page 98)
1 pound dried farfalle
1 tbsp olive oil
⁵/₈ cup white wine
1 tbsp pink peppercorns

4 ounces baby carrots
⁵/₈ cup heavy cream or
    fromage frais
salt and pepper

1 Peel and devein all of the shrimp. Thinly slice the sea bream. Melt the butter in a pan, add the sea bream, scallops, and shrimp, and cook for about 1–2 minutes.

2 Season with black pepper. Add the lemon juice and grated rind. Very carefully add the saffron powder or a few strands of saffron to the cooking juices (not to the seafood).

3 Remove the seafood from the pan, set aside and keep warm. Retain the juices.

4 Return the pan to the heat and add the vegetable stock. Bring to a boil and reduce by one-third. Add the vinegar and cook for 4 minutes, until reduced.

5 Bring a pan of salted water to a boil. Add the

farfalle and olive oil and cook until tender, but still firm to the bite. Drain and transfer to a warm plate and top with the seafood.

6 Add the wine, peppercorns, and carrots to the pan and reduce the sauce for 6 minutes. Add the cream or fromage frais and simmer for 2 minutes. Pour the sauce over the seafood and pasta and serve.

Seafood Lasagne

Serves 4

INGREDIENTS

1 pound finnan haddock, filleted, skin removed and flesh flaked	4 tbsp butter	1 pound precooked lasagne
4 ounces shrimp	3 leeks, very thinly sliced	$^2/_3$ cup freshly grated Parmesan cheese
4 ounces sole fillet, skin removed and flesh sliced	$^1/_2$ cup all-purpose flour	black pepper
juice of 1 lemon	$2^1/_3$ cups milk	
	2 tbsp clear honey	
	$1^3/_4$ cups grated mozzarella cheese	

1 Put the haddock fillet, shrimp, and sole fillet into a large bowl and season with black pepper to taste and a little lemon juice. Set aside while you start to make the sauce.

2 Melt the butter in a large saucepan. Add the leeks and cook, stirring occasionally, for 8 minutes. Add the flour and cook, stirring constantly, for 1 minute. Gradually stir in enough milk to make a thick, creamy sauce.

3 Blend in the honey and mozzarella cheese and cook for 3 minutes longer. Remove the pan from the heat and mix in the fish and shrimp.

4 Make alternate layers of fish sauce and lasagne in an ovenproof dish, finishing with a layer of fish sauce on top. Generously sprinkle the grated Parmesan cheese and bake in a preheated oven at 350°F for 30 minutes. Serve the lasagne immediately.

VARIATION

For a cider sauce, substitute 1 finely chopped shallot for the leeks, $1^1/_4$ cups cider, and $1^1/_4$ cups heavy cream for the milk and 1 tsp mustard for the honey.

For a Tuscan sauce, substitute 1 finely chopped fennel bulb for the leeks and omit the honey.

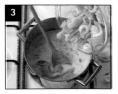

Spaghetti with Seafood Sauce

Serves 4

INGREDIENTS

8 ounces dried spaghetti,
   broken into 6-inch lengths
2 tbsp olive oil
1¼ cups chicken stock
1 tsp lemon juice
1 small cauliflower, cut into
   florets
2 carrots, thinly sliced
14 ounces snow peas

4 tbsp butter
1 onion, sliced
8 ounces zucchini, sliced
1 garlic clove, chopped
12 ounces frozen, cooked,
   peeled shrimp, defrosted
2 tbsp chopped fresh parsley
⅓ cup freshly grated
   Parmesan cheese

½ tsp paprika
salt and pepper
4 unpeeled, cooked shrimp,
   to garnish

1 Bring a pan of salted water to a boil. Add the spaghetti and 1 tbsp of the olive oil and cook until tender, but still firm to the bite. Drain and toss with the remaining olive oil, cover, and keep warm.

2 Bring the chicken stock and lemon juice to a boil. Add the cauliflower and carrots and cook for 3–4 minutes.

Remove from the pan and set aside. Add the snow peas to the pan and cook for 1–2 minutes. Set aside with the other vegetables.

3 Melt half of the butter in a skillet and sauté the onion and zucchini for about 3 minutes. Add the garlic and shrimp to the skillet and cook for a further 2–3 minutes, until thoroughly heated through.

Stir in the reserved vegetables and heat through. Season with salt and pepper to taste and stir in the remaining butter.

4 Transfer the pasta to a warm serving dish. Pour over the sauce and add the parsley. Toss well and sprinkle with the Parmesan and paprika, garnish with the unpeeled shrimp, and serve.

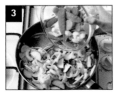

Macaroni & Shrimp Bake

Serves 4

INGREDIENTS

3 cups dried short-cut
macaroni
1 tbsp olive oil, plus extra
for brushing
6 tbsp butter, plus extra for
greasing
2 small fennel bulbs, thinly
sliced and fronds reserved

6 ounces mushrooms, thinly
sliced
6 ounces peeled, cooked
shrimp
pinch of cayenne pepper
1 1/4 cups Béchamel sauce (see
Cook's Tip)

2/3 cup freshly grated
Parmesan cheese
2 large tomatoes, sliced
1 tsp dried oregano
salt and pepper

1 Bring a saucepan of
salted water to a boil.
Add the pasta and oil and
cook until tender, but still
firm to the bite. Drain and
return to the pan. Add 2
tbsp of butter, cover, shake
the pan, and keep warm.

2 Melt the remaining
butter in a pan. Sauté
the fennel for 3–4 minutes.
Stir in the mushrooms and
cook for 2 minutes. Stir in
the shrimp, then remove
the pan from the heat.

3 Stir the pasta, cayenne
pepper and shrimp
mixture into the béchamel
sauce. Pour into a greased
ovenproof dish. Sprinkle
with the Parmesan cheese
and arrange the tomato
slices around the edge.
Brush the tomatoes with
olive oil and sprinkle the
oregano on top.

4 Bake in a preheated
oven at 350°F for
25 minutes, until golden
brown. Serve immediately.

COOK'S TIP

*For béchamel sauce, melt
2 tbsp butter. Stir in 1/4 cup
flour. Cook, stirring, for
2 minutes. Gradually, stir
in 1 1/4 cups warm milk.
Add 2 tbsp finely chopped
onion, 5 white peppercorns,
and 2 parsley sprigs, and
season with salt, dried
thyme, and grated nutmeg.
Simmer, stirring, for
15 minutes. Strain
before using.*

Pasta Packets

Serves 4

INGREDIENTS

1 pound dried fettuccine	1 pound 10 ounces large raw	$^1/_2$ cup dry white wine
$^5/_8$ cup pesto sauce (see	shrimp, peeled and	salt and pepper
page 12)	deveined	lemon wedges, to serve
4 tsp extra virgin olive oil	2 garlic cloves, crushed	

1 Cut out 4 × 12-inch squares of baking paper.

2 Bring a large saucepan of lightly salted water to a boil. Add the fettuccine and cook for 2–3 minutes, until just softened. Drain thoroughly, keep warm, and set aside.

3 Mix together the fettuccine and half of the pesto sauce. Spread out the paper squares and put 1 tsp olive oil in the middle of each. Divide the fettuccine between the squares, then divide the shrimp, and place on top of the fettuccine.

4 Mix together the remaining pesto sauce and the garlic and spoon it over the shrimp. Season each packet with salt and black pepper and sprinkle with the white wine.

5 Dampen the edges of the baking paper and wrap the packets loosely, twisting the edges to seal.

6 Place the packets on a cookie sheet and bake in a preheated oven at 400°F for about 10–15 minutes. Transfer the packets to 4 warm individual plates and serve with lemon wedges.

COOK'S TIP

Traditionally, these packets are designed to look like old-fashioned money bags. The resemblance is more effective with baking paper than with foil.

Farfallini Buttered Lobster

Serves 4

INGREDIENTS

2 1-pound, 9-ounce lobsters, split into halves	2 tbsp brandy	salt and pepper
juice and grated rind of 1 lemon	5 tbsp heavy cream or crème fraîche	TO GARNISH:
1/2 cup butter	1 pound dried farfallini	1 kiwi fruit, sliced
4 tbsp fresh white breadcrumbs	1 tbsp olive oil	4 large, unpeeled, cooked shrimp
	2/3 cup freshly grated Parmesan cheese	fresh dill sprigs

1 Carefully discard the stomach sac, vein, and gills from each lobster. Remove all the meat from the tail and chop. Crack the claws and legs, remove the meat, and chop. Transfer the meat to a bowl and add the lemon juice and rind.

2 Clean the shells and place in a warm oven at 325°F to dry out.

3 Melt 2 tbsp of the butter in a skillet. Add the breadcrumbs and fry for about 3 minutes, until crisp and golden brown.

4 Melt the remaining butter in a saucepan. Add the lobster meat and heat through gently. Add the brandy and cook for a further 3 minutes, then add the cream or crème fraîche, and season to taste.

5 Meanwhile, bring a large pan of lightly salted water to a boil. Add the farfallini and olive oil and cook for 12 minutes, until tender, but still firm to the bite. Drain and spoon the pasta into the lobster shells. Top with the buttered lobster and sprinkle with a little grated Parmesan cheese and the breadcrumbs. Broil for 2–3 minutes, until a light golden brown color.

6 Transfer the lobster shells to a warm serving dish, garnish with the, kiwi fruit, unpeeled shrimp, and dill sprigs, and serve.

Pasta Shells with Mussels

Serves 4–6

INGREDIENTS

2³/₄ pounds mussels
1 cup dry white wine
2 large onions, chopped
¹/₂ cup unsalted butter

6 large garlic cloves, finely
   chopped
5 tbsp chopped fresh parsley
1¹/₄ cups heavy cream
14 ounces dried pasta shells

1 tbsp olive oil
salt and pepper
crusty bread, to serve

1 Scrub and debeard the mussels under cold running water. Discard any that do not close when sharply tapped. Put the mussels into a large saucepan with the wine and half of the onions. Cover and cook over a medium heat until the shells open.

2 Remove the pan from the heat. Drain the mussels and reserve the cooking liquid. Discard any mussels that have not opened. Strain the cooking liquid and reserve.

3 Melt the butter in a pan and sauté the remaining onion until translucent. Stir in the garlic and cook for 1 minute. Gradually stir in the reserved cooking liquid, then the parsley and cream. Season and simmer.

4 Cook the pasta with the oil until just tender, but still firm to the bite. Drain, return to the pan, cover and keep warm.

5 Reserve a few mussels for the garnish and remove the remainder from their shells. Stir the shelled mussels into the cream sauce and warm briefly. Transfer the pasta to a serving dish. Pour the sauce over the pasta and toss to coat. Garnish with the reserved mussels and serve with bread.

COOK'S TIP

Pasta shells are ideal because the sauce collects in the cavities and impregnates the pasta with flavor.

Saffron Mussel Tagliatelle

Serves 4

INGREDIENTS

2¼ pounds mussels
⅝ cup white wine
1 medium onion, finely
  chopped
2 tbsp butter
2 garlic cloves, crushed
2 tsp cornstarch

1¼ cups heavy cream
pinch of saffron threads or
  saffron powder
1 egg yolk
juice of ½ lemon
1 pound dried tagliatelle
1 tbsp olive oil

salt and pepper
3 tbsp chopped fresh parsley,
  to garnish

1 Scrub and debeard the mussels under cold running water. Discard any that do not close when sharply tapped. Put the mussels in a pan with the wine and onion. Cover and cook over a high heat until the shells open.

2 Drain and reserve the cooking liquid. Discard any mussels that are still closed. Reserve a few mussels for the garnish and remove the remainder from their shells.

3 Strain the cooking liquid into a saucepan. Bring to a boil and reduce by about half. Remove the pan from the heat.

4 Melt the butter in a saucepan and fry the garlic for 2 minutes, until golden brown. Stir in the cornstarch and cook, stirring, for 1 minute. Gradually stir in the cooking liquid and the cream. Crush the saffron threads and add to the pan. Season to taste and simmer

for 2–3 minutes, until the sauce has thickened.

5 Stir in the egg yolk, lemon juice, and shelled mussels. Do not allow the mixture to boil.

6 Bring a pan of salted water to a boil. Add the pasta and oil and cook until tender. Drain and transfer to a serving dish. Add the mussel sauce and toss. Garnish with the parsley and reserved mussels and serve.

Baked Scallops with Pasta in Shells

Serves 4

INGREDIENTS

12 scallops
3 tbsp olive oil
3 cups small, dried whole-
    wheat pasta shells
5/8 cup fish stock

1 onion, chopped
juice of 2 lemons
5/8 cup heavy cream
2 cups freshly grated
    cheddar cheese

salt and pepper
crusty brown bread, to serve

1 Remove the scallops from their shells. Scrape off the skirt and the black intestinal thread. Reserve the white part (the flesh) and the orange part (the coral or roe). Carefully ease the flesh and coral from the shell with a short, but very strong knife.

2 Wash the shells thoroughly and dry them well. Put the shells on a cookie sheet, sprinkle lightly with about two-thirds of the olive oil, and set aside.

3 Meanwhile, bring a large saucepan of lightly salted water to a boil. Add the pasta shells and remaining olive oil and cook for about 12 minutes, until tender, but still firm to the bite. Drain and spoon about 1 ounce of pasta into each scallop shell.

4 Put the scallops, fish stock, and onion in an ovenproof dish and season to taste with pepper. Cover with foil and bake in a preheated oven at 350°F for 8 minutes.

5 Remove the dish from the oven. Remove the foil and, using a slotted spoon, transfer the scallops to the shells. Add 1 tbsp of the cooking liquid to each shell, together with a drizzle of lemon juice and a little cream, and top with the grated cheese.

6 Increase the oven temperature to 450°F and return the scallops to the oven for 4 minutes. Serve the scallops in their shells with crusty brown bread and butter.

Vermicelli with Clams

Serves 4

INGREDIENTS

14 ounces dried vermicelli,
spaghetti, or other long
pasta
2 tbsp olive oil
2 tbsp butter
2 onions, chopped
2 garlic cloves, chopped

2 7-ounce jars clams in water
$^1/_2$ cup white wine
4 tbsp chopped fresh parsley
$^1/_2$ tsp dried oregano
pinch of freshly grated
nutmeg
salt and pepper

TO GARNISH:
2 tbsp Parmesan cheese
shavings
fresh basil sprigs

1 Bring a large pan of lightly salted water to a boil. Add the pasta and half the olive oil and cook until tender, but still firm to the bite. Drain, return to the pan, and add the butter. Cover the pan, shake well, and keep warm.

2 Heat the remaining oil in a pan over a medium heat. Add the onions and sauté until they are translucent. Stir in the garlic and cook for 1 minute.

3 Strain the liquid from 1 jar of clams and add the liquid to the pan, with the wine. Stir, bring to simmering point, and simmer for 3 minutes. Drain the second jar of clams and discard the liquid.

4 Add the clams, parsley, and oregano to the pan and season with pepper and nutmeg. Lower the heat and cook until the sauce is completely heated through.

5 Transfer the pasta to a serving dish and pour over the sauce. Garnish and serve immediately.

COOK'S TIP

There are many different types of clams found along almost every coast in the world. Those traditionally used in this dish are the very tiny ones—only 1–2 inches across—known in Italy as vongole.

Squid & Macaroni Stew

Serves 4–6

INGREDIENTS

2 cups dried short-cut
  macaroni or other small
  pasta shapes
7 tbsp olive oil
2 onions, sliced
12 ounces prepared squid, cut
  into 1 1/2-inch strips

1 cup fish stock
5/8 cup red wine
12 ounces tomatoes, skinned
  and thinly sliced
2 tbsp tomato paste
1 tsp dried oregano
2 bay leaves

2 tbsp chopped fresh parsley
salt and pepper
crusty bread, to serve

1 Bring a large pan of
lightly salted water to a
boil. Add the pasta and
1 tbsp of the olive oil and
cook for 3 minutes. Drain
and keep warm.

2 Heat the remaining oil
in a pan and sauté the
onions until translucent.
Add the squid and stock
and simmer for 5 minutes.
Pour in the wine, tomatoes,
tomato paste, oregano, and
bay leaves. Bring the sauce
to a boil, season to taste,
and cook for 5 minutes.

3 Stir the pasta into the
pan, cover, and simmer
for about 10 minutes, or
until the squid and macaroni
are tender and the sauce has
thickened. If the sauce
remains too liquid, uncover
the pan and continue
cooking for a few minutes.

4 Discard the bay leaves.
Reserve a little parsley
and stir the remainder into
the pan. Transfer to a warm
serving dish and sprinkle
with the remaining parsley.
Serve with crusty bread.

COOK'S TIP

*To prepare squid, peel off the
outer skin, then cut off the
head and tentacles. Extract
the transparent flat oval bone
from the body and discard.
Remove the sac of black ink,
then turn the body sac inside
out. Wash in cold water. Cut
off the tentacles and discard
the rest; wash thoroughly.*

Vegetables & Salads

The pasta recipes in this chapter offer something special for every occasion: filling vegetarian suppers, unusual vegetable side dishes, main courses, and side salads. You could even take many of the salads on a picnic and, of course, they are perfect as accompaniments for summer barbecues.

Some are classic dishes, such as Fettuccine all'Alfredo, Spaghetti Olio e Aglio, Paglia e Fieno, and Pasta & Herring Salad. Others are imaginative and sometimes surprising new combinations of vegetables and pasta. Try Mediterranean Spaghetti, Spinach & Wild Mushroom Lasagne, Ravioli with Vegetable Stuffing, and Rare Beef Pasta Salad for a family meal, while Linguine with Braised Fennel, Goat Cheese with Penne & Walnut Salad, and Pasta & Garlic Mayo Salad make superb side dishes to get the taste buds tingling.

Fettuccine all'Alfredo

Serves 4

INGREDIENTS

2 tbsp butter
⅞ cup heavy cream
1 pound fresh fettuccine
1 tbsp olive oil

1 cup freshly grated Parmesan
cheese, plus extra
to serve

pinch of freshly grated
nutmeg
salt and pepper
fresh parsley sprigs, to garnish

1 Put the butter and ⅝ cup of the cream in a large saucepan and bring the mixture to a boil over a medium heat. Reduce the heat and then simmer gently for about 1½ minutes, or until slightly thickened.

2 Meanwhile, bring a large saucepan of lightly salted water to a boil. Add the fettuccine and olive oil and cook for 2–3 minutes, until tender, but still firm to the bite. Drain the fettuccine and then pour the cream and butter sauce over the top.

3 Toss the fettuccine in the sauce over a low heat until thoroughly coated.

4 Add the remaining cream, the Parmesan cheese, and nutmeg to the fettuccine mixture and season to taste with salt and pepper. Toss thoroughly to coat while heating through.

5 Transfer the fettuccine mixture to a warm serving plate and garnish with the fresh sprig of parsley. Serve immediately, with extra grated Parmesan cheese on the side.

VARIATION

This classic Roman dish is often served with the addition of strips of ham and fresh peas. Add 2 cups shelled cooked peas and 6 ounces ham strips with the Parmesan cheese in step 4.

Macaroni Bake

Serves 4

INGREDIENTS
---

4 cups dried short-cut
  macaroni
1 tbsp olive oil
4 tbsp beef drippings
1 pound potatoes, thinly sliced

1 pound onions, sliced
2 cups grated mozzarella
  cheese
⅝ cup heavy cream
salt and pepper

crusty brown bread and butter,
  to serve

1 Bring a large saucepan of lightly salted water to a boil. Add the macaroni and olive oil and cook for about 12 minutes, until tender, but still firm to the bite. Drain the macaroni thoroughly, set aside, and keep warm.

2 Melt the drippings in a large flameproof casserole, then remove from the heat.

3 Make alternate layers of potatoes, onions, macaroni, and grated cheese in the dish, seasoning well with salt and pepper between each layer and finishing with a layer of cheese on top. Finally, pour the cream over the top layer of cheese.

4 Bake in a preheated oven at 400°F for 25 minutes. Remove the dish from the oven and carefully brown the top under a broiler.

5 Serve the bake straight from the dish with lots of crusty brown bread and butter, as a main course. Alternatively, you could serve the dish as a vegetable accompaniment with your favorite main course.

VARIATION

For a stronger flavor, use mozzarella affumicata, a smoked version of this cheese, or Swiss cheese instead of the mozzarella.

Creamy Pasta & Broccoli

Serves 4

INGREDIENTS

4 tbsp butter
1 large onion, finely chopped
1 pound dried ribbon pasta
1 pound broccoli, broken into
   florets

$5/8$ cup boiling vegetable stock
1 tbsp all-purpose flour
$5/8$ cup light cream
$1/2$ cup grated mozzarella
   cheese

freshly grated nutmeg
salt and white pepper
fresh apple slices, to garnish

1 Melt half of the butter in a large saucepan over a medium heat. Add the onion and sauté for 4 minutes.

2 Add the broccoli and pasta to the pan and cook, stirring constantly, for 2 minutes. Add the vegetable stock, bring back to a boil, and simmer for a further 12 minutes. Season well with salt and white pepper.

3 Meanwhile, melt the remaining butter in a saucepan over a medium heat. Sprinkle in the flour and cook, stirring constantly, for 2 minutes. Gradually stir in the cream and bring to simmering point, but do not boil. Add the grated cheese and season with salt and a little freshly grated nutmeg.

4 Drain the pasta and broccoli mixture and pour in the cheese sauce. Cook, stirring occasionally, for 2 minutes. Transfer the pasta and broccoli mixture to a warm serving dish, and serve garnished with slices of fresh apple.

VARIATION

This dish would also be delicious and look just as colorful made with Cape broccoli, which is actually a purple variety of cauliflower and not broccoli at all.

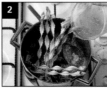

Paglia e Fieno

Serves 4

INGREDIENTS

4 tbsp butter
1 pound fresh peas, shelled
7/8 cup heavy cream
1 pound mixed fresh green
    and white spaghetti or
    tagliatelle

1 tbsp olive oil
2/3 cup freshly grated
    Parmesan cheese, plus extra
    to serve
pinch of freshly grated
    nutmeg

salt and pepper

1 Melt the butter in a large saucepan. Add the peas and cook, over a low heat, for 2–3 minutes.

2 Using a measuring pitcher, pour 5/8 cup of the cream into the pan, bring to a boil, and simmer for 1–1½ minutes, until slightly thickened. Remove the pan from the heat.

3 Meanwhile, bring a large pan of lightly salted water to a boil. Add the spaghetti or tagliatelle

and olive oil and cook for 2–3 minutes, until just tender, but still firm to the bite. Remove the pan from the heat, drain the pasta thoroughly, and return to the pan.

4 Add the peas and cream sauce to the pasta. Return the pan to the heat and add the remaining cream and the grated Parmesan cheese. Season to taste with salt, black pepper, and a pinch of grated nutmeg.

5 Using 2 forks, gently toss the pasta to coat with the peas and cream sauce, while it is heating through.

6 Transfer the pasta to a serving dish and serve immediately, with extra Parmesan cheese.

Green Tagliatelle with Garlic

Serves 4

INGREDIENTS

2 tbsp walnut oil
1 bunch scallions, sliced
2 garlic cloves, thinly sliced
3¹/4 cups sliced mushrooms
1 pound fresh green and
    white tagliatelle
1 tbsp olive oil

8 ounces frozen spinach,
    thawed and drained
¹/2 cup full-fat soft cheese
    with garlic and herbs
4 tbsp light cream
¹/2 cup chopped, unsalted
    pistachio nuts
salt and pepper

TO GARNISH:
2 tbsp shredded fresh basil
fresh basil sprigs
Italian bread, to serve

1 Heat the walnut oil in a large skillet. Add the scallions and garlic and sauté for 1 minute, until just softened.

2 Add the mushrooms to the pan, stir well, cover, and cook over a low heat for about 5 minutes, until softened.

3 Meanwhile, bring a large saucepan of lightly salted water to a boil. Add the tagliatelle and

olive oil and cook for 3–5 minutes, until tender, but still firm to the bite. Drain the tagliatelle thoroughly and return to the saucepan.

4 Add the spinach to the skillet and heat through for about 1–2 minutes. Add the cheese to the pan and allow to melt slightly. Stir in the cream and cook, stirring occasionally and without allowing the mixture to

come to a boil, until it is heated through.

5 Pour the sauce over the pasta, season to taste, and mix well. Heat through gently, stirring constantly, for 2–3 minutes.

6 Transfer the pasta to a serving dish and sprinkle with the pistachio nuts and shredded basil. Garnish with the basil sprigs and serve.

Spaghetti Olio e Aglio

Serves 4

INGREDIENTS

$^1/_2$ cup olive oil
3 garlic cloves, crushed
1 pound fresh spaghetti

3 tbsp roughly chopped fresh
parsley

salt and pepper

1 Reserve 1 tbsp of the olive oil and heat the remainder in a medium saucepan. Add the garlic and a pinch of salt and cook over a low heat, stirring constantly, until golden brown, then remove the pan from the heat. Do not allow the garlic to burn as it will taint its flavor. (If it does burn, you will have to start all over again!)

2 Meanwhile, bring a large saucepan of lightly salted water to a boil. Add the spaghetti and remaining olive oil and cook for 2–3 minutes, until tender, but still firm to the bite. Drain the spaghetti thoroughly and return to the pan.

3 Add the oil and garlic mixture to the spaghetti and toss to coat thoroughly. Season with pepper, add the chopped fresh parsley, and toss to coat again.

4 Transfer the spaghetti to a warm serving dish and serve immediately.

COOK'S TIP

It is worth buying the best-quality olive oil for dishes such as this one which makes a feature of its flavor. Extra virgin oil is produced from the first pressing and has the lowest acidity. It is more expensive than other types of olive oil, but has the finest flavor. Virgin olive oil is slightly more acidic, but is also well flavored. Oil simply labeled pure has usually been heat-treated and refined by mechanical means and, consequently, lacks character and flavor.

Patriotic Pasta

Serves 4

INGREDIENTS

4 cups dried farfalle	1 pound cherry tomatoes	salt and pepper
4 tbsp olive oil	3 ounces arugula	Pecorino cheese, to garnish

1 Bring a large saucepan of lightly salted water to a boil. Add the farfalle and 1 tbsp of the olive oil and cook until tender, but still firm to the bite. Drain the farfalle thoroughly and return to the pan.

2 Cut the cherry tomatoes in half and trim the arugula, using a sharp knife.

3 Heat the remaining olive oil in a large saucepan. Add the tomatoes and cook for 1 minute. Add the farfalle and the arugula and gently mix. Heat through and season to taste.

4 Meanwhile, using a vegetable peeler, shave thin slices of Pecorino cheese.

5 Transfer the farfalle and vegetables to a warm serving dish. Garnish with the Pecorino cheese shavings and serve immediately.

COOK'S TIP

Pecorino cheese is a hard ewe's milk cheese which resembles Parmesan and is often used for grating over a variety of dishes. It has a sharp flavor and is used only in small quantities.

COOK'S TIP

Arugula is a small plant with irregular-shaped leaves rather like those of turnip greens. The flavor is distinctively peppery and slightly reminiscent of radish. It has always been popular in Italy, both in salads and for serving with pasta, and has recently enjoyed a revival in the United States and Britain.

Mediterranean Spaghetti

Serves 4

INGREDIENTS

2 tbsp olive oil
1 large, red onion, chopped
2 garlic cloves, crushed
1 tbsp lemon juice
4 baby eggplants, quartered
2 1/2 cups sieved tomatoes
2 tsp superfine sugar

2 tbsp tomato paste
14 ounce can artichoke hearts, drained and halved
1 cup pitted black olives
12 ounces dried spaghetti
2 tbsp butter
salt and pepper

fresh basil sprigs, to garnish
olive bread, to serve

1 Heat 1 tbsp of the olive oil in a large skillet. Add the onion, garlic, lemon juice, and eggplant and cook over a low heat for 4–5 minutes, until the onion and eggplant are lightly golden brown.

2 Pour in the sieved tomatoes, season to taste with salt and black pepper, and stir in the sugar and tomato paste. Bring to a boil, lower the heat slightly, and then simmer, stirring occasionally, for about 20 minutes.

3 Carefully stir in the artichoke hearts and black olives and cook for 5 minutes.

4 Meanwhile, bring a large saucepan of lightly salted water to a boil. Add the spaghetti and the remaining olive oil and cook for 7–8 minutes, until the pasta is tender, but still firm to the bite.

5 Drain the spaghetti thoroughly and toss with the butter. Transfer to a serving dish.

6 Pour the vegetable sauce over the spaghetti, garnish with the sprigs of fresh basil, and serve immediately with olive bread.

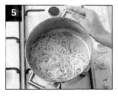

Spinach & Mushroom Lasagne

Serves 4

INGREDIENTS
---

8 tbsp butter, plus extra for
   greasing
2 garlic cloves, finely chopped
4 ounces shallots
8 ounces exotic mushrooms,
   such as chanterelles

1 pound spinach, cooked,
   drained and finely chopped
2 cups grated cheddar cheese
$1/4$ tsp freshly grated nutmeg
1 tsp chopped fresh basil
2 ounces all-purpose flour
$2^1/2$ cups hot milk

$2/3$ cup grated Cheshire
   cheese
salt and pepper
8 sheets precooked lasagne

---

1 Lightly grease an ovenproof dish.

2 Melt 4 tbsp of the butter in a saucepan. Add the garlic, shallots, and mushrooms and sauté over a low heat for 3 minutes. Stir in the spinach, cheddar cheese, nutmeg, and basil. Season well and set aside.

3 Melt the remaining butter in another saucepan. Add the flour and cook, stirring constantly, for 1 minute. Gradually stir in the hot milk, whisking constantly until smooth. Stir in $1/4$ cup of the Cheshire cheese and season to taste.

4 Spread half of the mushroom and spinach mixture over the base of the prepared dish. Cover with a layer of lasagne and then with half of the cheese sauce. Repeat the process and sprinkle with the remaining Cheshire cheese. Bake in a preheated oven at 400°F for 30 minutes, until golden brown.

VARIATION

Substitute 4 bell peppers for the spinach. Roast in a preheated oven at 400°F for 20 minutes. Rub off the skins under cold water, seed, and chop before using.

Ravioli with Vegetable Stuffing

Serves 4

INGREDIENTS

1 pound Basic Pasta Dough
  (see page 4)
1 tbsp olive oil
6 tbsp butter
⁵/₈ cup light cream
1 cup freshly grated
  Parmesan cheese

STUFFING:
2 large eggplant
3 large zucchini
6 large tomatoes
1 large green bell pepper
1 large red bell pepper
3 garlic cloves
1 large onion

¹/₂ cup olive oil
2 ounces tomato paste
¹/₂ tsp chopped fresh basil
salt and pepper

1 To make the stuffing, cut the eggplant and zucchini into 1-inch chunks. Sprinkle the eggplant with salt and set aside for 20 minutes. Rinse the eggplant and drain thoroughly.

2 Blanch the tomatoes in boiling water for 2 minutes. Drain, skin, and chop the flesh. Core and seed the bell peppers and cut into 1-inch pieces. Chop the garlic and onion.

3 Heat the oil in a saucepan. Add the garlic and onion and sauté for 3 minutes. Stir in the eggplant, zucchini, tomatoes, bell peppers, tomato paste, and basil. Season with salt and pepper to taste, cover, and leave to simmer for about 20 minutes, stirring frequently.

4 Roll out the pasta dough and cut out 3-inch rounds. Put a spoonful of the vegetable

stuffing onto each round. Dampen the edges and fold the pasta rounds over, pressing together to seal.

5 Bring a pan of salted water to a boil.and cook the ravioli with the for 3–4 minutes. Drain and transfer to a greased ovenproof dish, dotting with butter. Pour in the cream and sprinkle with the Parmesan cheese. Bake in a preheated oven at 400°F for 20 minutes.

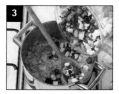

Zucchini & Eggplant Lasagne

Serves 6

INGREDIENTS

2 ¼ pounds eggplant
8 tbsp olive oil
2 tbsp garlic and herb butter
1 pound zucchini, sliced
2 cups grated
   mozzarella cheese
2 ½ cups sieved tomatoes

6 sheets precooked green
   lasagne
2 ½ cups Béchamel sauce (see
   page 166)
⅔ cup freshly grated
   Parmesan cheese
1 tsp dried oregano

salt and pepper

1 Thinly slice the eggplant and place in a colander. Sprinkle with salt and set aside for 20 minutes. Rinse and pat dry with paper towels.

2 Heat 4 tbsp of the olive oil in a large skillet. Fry half the eggplant slices over a low heat for 6–7 minutes, until golden. Drain on paper towels. Repeat with the remaining oil and eggplant slices.

3 Melt the garlic and herb butter in the skillet. Add the zucchini and fry for 5–6 minutes, until golden brown all over. Drain on paper towels.

4 Place half the eggplant and zucchini slices in a large ovenproof dish. Season with pepper and sprinkle with half the mozzarella cheese. Spoon half the sieved tomatoes over the cheese and top

with 3 sheets of lasagne. Repeat the process, ending with a layer of lasagne.

5 Top with the béchamel sauce and sprinkle the Parmesan cheese and oregano. Put the dish on a cookie sheet and bake in a preheated oven at 425°F for 30–35 minutes, until golden brown. Serve immediately.

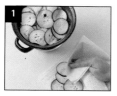

Pasta & Bean Casserole

Serves 6

INGREDIENTS

1¼ cups dried navy beans,
    soaked overnight and
    drained
8 ounces dried penne
6 tbsp olive oil
3½ cups vegetable stock
2 large onions, sliced
2 garlic cloves, chopped
2 bay leaves

1 tsp dried oregano
1 tsp dried thyme
5 tbsp red wine
2 tbsp tomato paste
2 celery stalks, sliced
1 fennel bulb, sliced
1⅝ cups sliced mushrooms
8 ounces tomatoes, sliced
1 tsp dark brown sugar

4 tbsp dry white breadcrumbs
salt and pepper
salad greens and crusty bread,
    to serve

1 Put the navy beans in a large saucepan and add sufficient cold water to cover. Bring to a boil and continue to boil vigorously for 20 minutes. Drain, set aside, and keep warm.

2 Bring a large saucepan of lightly salted water to a boil. Add the penne and 1 tbsp of the olive oil and cook for about 3 minutes. Drain the pasta, set aside, and keep warm.

3 Put the beans in a large, flameproof casserole. Add the vegetable stock and stir in the remaining olive oil, the onions, garlic, bay leaves, oregano, thyme, wine, and tomato paste. Bring to a boil, then cover, and cook in a preheated oven at 350°F for 2 hours.

4 Add the penne, celery, fennel, mushrooms, and tomatoes to the casserole and season to taste with salt and pepper. Stir in the sugar and top with the breadcrumbs. Cover the dish and cook in the oven for 1 hour.

5 Serve hot with salad greens and crusty bread.

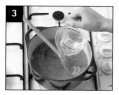

Creamed Spaghetti & Mushrooms

Serves 4

INGREDIENTS

4 tbsp butter

2 tbsp olive oil

6 shallots, sliced

6 cups sliced
   button mushrooms

1 tsp all-purpose flour

$^5/_8$ cup heavy cream

2 tbsp port

4 ounces sun-dried
   tomatoes, chopped

freshly grated nutmeg

1 pound dried spaghetti

1 tbsp freshly chopped parsley

salt and pepper

6 triangles of fried white
   bread, to serve

---

1 Heat the butter and 1 tbsp of the oil in a large saucepan. Add the shallots and cook for 3 minutes. Add the mushrooms and cook over a low heat for 2 minutes. Season with salt and black pepper, sprinkle in the flour, and cook, stirring constantly, for 1 minute.

2 Gradually stir in the cream and port, add the sun-dried tomatoes and a pinch of grated nutmeg, and cook over a low heat for 8 minutes.

3 Bring a large saucepan of lightly salted water to a boil. Add the spaghetti and remaining olive oil and cook for 12–14 minutes, until tender but still firm to the bite.

4 Drain the spaghetti and return to the pan. Add the mushroom sauce and cook for 3 minutes. Transfer the spaghetti and mushroom sauce to a large serving plate and sprinkle with chopped parsley. Serve with crispy triangles of fried bread.

VARIATION

Non-vegetarians could add 4 ounces prosciutto, cut into thin strips and heated gently in 2 tbsp butter, to the pasta along with the mushroom sauce.

Vegetable Pasta Stir-fry

Serves 4

INGREDIENTS

14 ounces dried whole-wheat
    pasta shells or other short
    pasta shapes
1 tbsp olive oil
2 carrots, thinly sliced
4 ounces baby corncobs
3 tbsp corn oil
1-inch piece fresh ginger root,
    thinly sliced
1 large onion, thinly sliced

1 garlic clove, thinly sliced
3 celery stalks, thinly sliced
1 small red bell pepper, cored,
    seeded, and cut into
    matchstick strips
1 small green bell pepper,
    cored, seeded, and cut into
    matchstick strips
1 tsp cornstarch
2 tbsp water

3 tbsp soy sauce
3 tbsp dry sherry
1 tsp clear honey
a dash of hot pepper sauce
    (optional)
salt

1 Bring a large saucepan of lightly salted water to a boil. Add the pasta and olive oil and cook until tender, but still firm to the bite. Drain, return to the pan, and keep warm.

2 Bring a saucepan of lightly salted water to a boil. Add the carrots and corncobs and cook for 2 minutes. Drain, rinse in cold water, and drain again.

3 Heat the corn oil in a preheated wok or large skillet. Add the ginger root and stir-fry over a medium heat for 1 minute to flavor the oil. Remove the ginger from the oil with a slotted spoon and discard.

4 Add the onion, garlic, celery, and bell peppers to the wok or skillet and stir-fry for 2 minutes. Add the carrots and baby corncobs and stir-fry for 2 minutes. Stir in the pasta.

5 Mix together the cornstarch and water to make a smooth paste. Stir in the soy sauce, sherry, and honey. Pour the cornstarch mixture into the pasta and cook, stirring occasionally, for 2 minutes. Stir in a dash of pepper sauce, if liked. Transfer to a serving dish and serve.

Macaroni & Corn Pancakes

Serves 4

INGREDIENTS

2 corncobs
4 tbsp butter
4 ounces red bell peppers,
  cored, seeded, and finely
  diced
$2^1/2$ cups dried short-
  cut macaroni

$^5/8$ cup heavy cream
$^1/4$ cup all-purpose flour
4 egg yolks
4 tbsp olive oil
salt and pepper

TO SERVE:
oyster mushrooms
fried leeks

1 Bring a saucepan of water to a boil, add the corncobs and cook for about 8 minutes. Drain and rinse under cold running water for 3 minutes. Carefully cut away the kernels onto paper towels and set aside to dry.

2 Melt 2 tbsp of the butter in a skillet. Add the bell peppers and cook over a low heat, stirring occasionally, for 4 minutes. Drain thoroughly and pat dry with paper towels.

3 Bring a large pan of lightly salted water to a boil. Add the macaroni and cook for 12 minutes, until tender, but still firm to the bite. Drain the macaroni and leave to cool in cold water.

4 Beat together the cream, flour, a pinch of salt, and the egg yolks in a bowl until smooth. Add the corn and bell peppers to the cream and egg mixture. Drain the macaroni and toss into the corn and

cream mixture. Season well with black pepper to taste.

5 Heat the remaining butter with the oil in a large skillet. Drop spoonfuls of the mixture into the pan and press down until the mixture forms a flat pancake. Fry until golden on both sides, and all the mixture is used up. Serve immediately with oyster mushrooms and fried leeks.

Vermicelli Flan

Serves 4

INGREDIENTS

---

6 tbsp butter, plus extra,
  for greasing
8 ounces dried vermicelli or
  spaghetti
1 tbsp olive oil
1 onion, chopped
5 ounces button mushrooms

1 green bell pepper, cored,
  seeded, and sliced into thin
  rings
$5/8$ cup milk
3 eggs, lightly beaten
2 tbsp heavy cream
1 tsp dried oregano

freshly grated nutmeg
1 tbsp freshly grated
  Parmesan cheese
salt and pepper
tomato and basil salad,
  to serve

---

1 Grease the base and sides of an 8-inch loose-based flan pan with butter.

2 Bring a large pan of lightly salted water to a boil. Add the vermicelli and olive oil and cook until tender, but still firm to the bite. Drain and toss in 2 tbsp of the butter.

3 Press the pasta onto the base and around the sides of the flan pan to make a flan case.

4 Melt the remaining butter in a skillet. Add the onion and sauté until it is translucent.

5 Add the mushrooms and bell pepper rings to the skillet and cook, stirring and turning constantly, for 2–3 minutes. Spoon the onion, mushroom and bell peppers into the flan case and press down evenly over the base.

6 Beat together the milk, eggs, and cream, stir in the oregano, and season to taste with nutmeg and black pepper. Carefully pour the mixture over the vegetables and sprinkle with the cheese.

7 Bake the flan in a preheated oven at 350°F for 40–45 minutes, until the filling has set.

8 Slide the flan out of the pan and serve warm with a tomato and basil salad.

Fettuccine with Olive, Garlic, & Walnut Sauce

Serves 4–6

INGREDIENTS

---

2 thick slices whole-wheat
    bread, crusts removed
1¼ cups milk
2½ cups shelled walnuts
2 garlic cloves, crushed
1 cup pitted black olives

⅔ cup freshly grated
    Parmesan cheese
8 tbsp extra virgin olive oil
⅝ cup heavy cream
1 pound fresh fettuccine
salt and pepper

2–3 tbsp chopped fresh
    parsley

---

1 Put the bread in a shallow dish, pour the milk over it, and set aside to soak until the liquid has been absorbed.

2 Spread the walnuts out on a cookie sheet and toast in a preheated oven at 375°F for about 5 minutes, until golden. Set aside to cool.

3 Put the soaked bread, walnuts, garlic, olives, Parmesan cheese, and 6 tbsp of the olive oil in a food processor and purée. Season to taste with a little salt and black pepper and stir in the cream.

4 Bring a large pan of lightly salted water to a boil. Add the fettuccine and 1 tablespoon of the remaining oil and cook for 2–3 minutes, until tender but still firm to the bite. Drain the pasta and toss with the remaining olive oil, until well combined.

5 Divide the fettuccine between individual plates and spoon the olive, garlic, and walnut sauce on top. Sprinkle with the fresh parsley and serve.

Linguine with Braised Fennel

Serves 4

INGREDIENTS

6 fennel bulbs
⁵/₈ cup vegetable stock
2 tbsp butter
6 slices bacon, diced
6 shallots, quartered

¹/₄ cup all-purpose flour
7 tbsp heavy cream
1 tbsp Madeira

1 pound dried linguine
1 tbsp olive oil
salt and pepper

1 Trim the fennel bulbs, then gently peel off and reserve the first layer of the bulbs. Cut the bulbs into quarters and put them in a large saucepan, together with the vegetable stock and the reserved outer layers. Bring to a boil, lower the heat, and simmer for 5 minutes.

2 Using a slotted spoon, transfer the fennel to a large dish. Discard the outer layers of the fennel bulb. Bring the vegetable stock to a boil and allow to reduce by half. Set aside.

3 Melt the butter in a skillet. Add the bacon and shallots and fry for 4 minutes. Add the flour, reduced stock, cream, and Madeira and cook, stirring constantly, for 3 minutes, until the sauce is smooth. Season to taste and pour over the fennel.

4 Bring a large saucepan of lightly salted water to a boil. Add the linguine and olive oil and cook for 10 minutes, until tender, but still firm to the bite. Drain and transfer to a deep ovenproof dish.

5 Add the fennel and sauce and braise in a preheated oven at 350°F for 20 minutes. Serve immediately from the dish.

COOK'S TIP

Fennel will keep in the salad drawer of the refrigerator for 2–3 days, but it is best eaten as fresh as possible. Cut surfaces turn brown quickly, so do not prepare it too much in advance of cooking.

Baked Eggplant with Pasta

Serves 4

INGREDIENTS

8 ounces dried penne or other short pasta shapes
4 tbsp olive oil, plus extra for brushing
2 eggplant
1 large onion, chopped

2 garlic cloves, crushed
14 ounce can chopped tomatoes
2 tsp dried oregano
2 ounces mozzarella cheese, thinly sliced

$^1/_3$ cup freshly grated Parmesan cheese
2 tbsp dry breadcrumbs
salt and pepper
salad greens, to serve

1 Bring a pan of salted water to a boil. Add the pasta and 1 tbsp of the olive oil and cook until tender, but still firm to the bite. Drain and keep warm.

2 Cut the eggplant in half lengthwise and score around the inside, being careful not to pierce the shells. Scoop out the flesh with a spoon. Brush the insides of the shells with olive oil. Chop the flesh and set aside.

3 Sauté the onion in the remaining oil until translucent. Add the garlic and cook for 1 minute. Add the chopped eggplant and cook for 5 minutes. Add the tomatoes and oregano and season to taste. Bring to a boil and simmer until thickened. Remove from the heat and stir in the pasta.

4 Brush a cookie sheet with oil and arrange the eggplant shells in a single layer. Divide half the tomato and pasta mixture between them. Sprinkle the mozzarella on, then pile the remaining tomato and pasta mixture on top. Mix the Parmesan cheese and breadcrumbs together and sprinkle over the top.

5 Bake in a preheated oven at 400°F for 25 minutes, until the topping is golden brown. Serve hot with salad greens.

Pasta with Green Vegetable Sauce

Serves 4

INGREDIENTS

2 cups dried gemelli or other
   pasta shapes
1 tbsp olive oil
1 head green broccoli, cut
   into florets
2 zucchini, sliced
8 ounces asparagus spears

4 ounces snow peas
4 ounces frozen peas
2 tbsp butter
3 tbsp vegetable stock
4 tbsp heavy cream
freshly grated nutmeg
2 tbsp chopped fresh parsley

2 tbsp freshly grated
   Parmesan cheese
salt and pepper

1 Bring a large saucepan of lightly salted water to a boil. Add the pasta and olive oil and cook until tender, but still firm to the bite. Drain, return to the pan, cover, and keep warm.

2 Steam the broccoli, zucchini, asparagus spears, and snow peas over a pan of boiling salted water until they are just beginning to soften. Remove from the heat and rinse in cold water. Drain thoroughly, and set aside.

3 Bring a small pan of lightly salted water to a boil. Add the frozen peas and cook for 3 minutes. Drain the peas, rinse in cold water, and then drain again. Set aside with the other vegetables.

4 Put the butter and vegetable stock in a pan over a medium heat. Add all of the vegetables, reserving a few of the asparagus spears, and toss carefully with a wooden spoon until they have

heated through, taking care not to break them up.

5 Stir in the cream and heat through without bringing to a boil. Add the seasoning and nutmeg.

6 Transfer the pasta to a warmed serving dish and stir in the chopped parsley. Spoon the vegetable sauce on top and sprinkle with Parmesan. Arrange the reserved asparagus spears in a pattern on top and serve.

Niçoise with Pasta Shells

Serves 4

INGREDIENTS

12 ounces dried small pasta
  shells
1 tbsp olive oil
4 ounces green beans
1³/4 ounce can anchovies,
  drained
¹/8 cup milk
2 small crisp lettuce heads

1 pound or 3 large beef
  tomatoes
4 hard-cooked eggs
8 ounce can tuna, drained
1 cup pitted black olives
salt and pepper

VINAIGRETTE DRESSING:
¹/4 cup extra virgin olive oil
¹/8 cup white wine vinegar
1 tsp wholegrain mustard
salt and pepper

1 Bring a large saucepan of lightly salted water to a boil. Add the pasta and the olive oil and cook until tender, but still firm to the bite. Drain and rinse in cold water.

2 Bring a small saucepan of lightly salted water to a boil. Add the beans and cook for 10–12 minutes, until tender, but still firm to the bite. Drain, rinse in cold water, drain thoroughly once more, and then set aside.

3 Put the anchovies in a shallow bowl, cover with the milk, and set aside for 10 minutes. Meanwhile, tear the lettuce into large pieces. Blanch the tomatoes in boiling water for 1–2 minutes, then drain, skin, and roughly chop the flesh. Shell the eggs and cut into quarters. Cut the tuna into large chunks.

4 Drain the anchovies and the pasta. Put all of the salad ingredients, the beans, and the olives into a large bowl and gently mix together.

5 To make the vinaigrette dressing, beat together all the ingredients and keep in the refrigerator until required. Just before serving, pour the vinaigrette dressing over the salad.

Herring & Pasta Salad

Serves 4

INGREDIENTS
---

9 ounces dried pasta shells
5 tbsp olive oil
14 ounces rollmop herrings in
    water
6 boiled potatoes

2 large tart apples
2 baby frisée lettuces
2 baby beets
4 hard-cooked eggs
6 pickled onions

6 dill pickles
2 tbsp capers
3 tbsp tarragon vinegar
salt and pepper

---

1 Bring a large saucepan of lightly salted water to a boil. Add the pasta and 1 tbsp of the olive oil and cook until tender, but still firm to the bite. Drain the pasta thoroughly and rinse in cold water.

2 Cut the herrings, potatoes, apples, frisée lettuces, and beets into small pieces. Put all of these ingredients into a large salad bowl.

3 Drain the pasta thoroughly and add to the salad bowl. Toss lightly to mix the pasta and herring mixture together.

4 Carefully shell and slice the eggs. Garnish the salad with the slices of egg, pickled onions, dill pickles, and capers, sprinkle with the remaining olive oil and the tarragon vinegar, and serve immediately.

COOK'S TIP

Store this salad, without the dressing, in a container in the refrigerator.

COOK'S TIP

Tarragon vinegar is available from most supermarkets, but you can easily make your own. Add a bunch of fresh tarragon to a bottle of white or red wine vinegar and leave to infuse for 48 hours. It is important to ensure that the tarragon is as fresh as possible and to discard any blemished leaves.

Neapolitan Seafood Salad with Campanelle

Serves 4

INGREDIENTS

1 pound prepared squid, cut into strips
1 pound 10 ounces cooked mussels
1 pound cooked cockles in water
$^5/_8$ cup white wine
$1^1/_4$ cups olive oil

2 cups dried campanelle or other small pasta shapes
juice of 1 lemon
1 bunch chives, snipped
1 bunch fresh parsley, finely chopped
4 large tomatoes, quartered or sliced

mixed salad greens
salt and pepper
sprig of fresh basil, to garnish

---

1 Put all of the seafood into a large bowl, pour in the wine and half the olive oil, and set aside for 6 hours.

2 Put the seafood mixture into a saucepan and simmer over a low heat for 10 minutes. Set aside to cool.

3 Bring a large saucepan of lightly salted water to a boil. Add the pasta and 1 tbsp of the remaining olive oil and cook until tender, but still firm to the bite. Drain thoroughly and rinse in cold water.

4 Strain off about half of the cooking liquid from the seafood and discard the rest. Mix in the lemon juice, chives, parsley, and the remaining olive oil. Season to taste with salt and pepper. Drain the pasta and add to the seafood.

5 Slice or cut the tomatoes into quarters. Shred the salad greens and arrange them on the base of a salad bowl. Spoon in the seafood salad and garnish with the quartered or sliced tomatoes and a sprig of basil.

Pasta Salad with Red & White Cabbage

Serves 4

INGREDIENTS

2¼ cups dried short-
  cut macaroni
5 tbsp olive oil
1 large red cabbage, shredded

1 large white cabbage,
  shredded
2 large apples, diced
9 ounces cooked smoked
  bacon or ham, diced

8 tbsp wine vinegar
1 tbsp sugar
salt and pepper

1 Bring a large pan of salted water to a boil. Add the macaroni and 1 tablespoon of the olive oil and cook until tender, but still firm to the bite. Drain the pasta, then rinse in cold water. Drain the pasta again and set aside.

2 Bring a large pan of lightly salted water to a boil. Add the shredded red cabbage and cook for 5 minutes. Drain thoroughly and set aside to cool.

3 Bring a large epan of lightly salted water to a boil. Add the white cabbage and cook for 5 minutes. Drain thoroughly and set aside to cool.

4 Mix together the pasta, red cabbage, and apple. Mix together the white cabbage and bacon or ham.

5 In a small bowl, mix together the remaining oil, the vinegar, and sugar and season to taste with salt and pepper. Pour the

dressing over each of the 2 cabbage mixtures and, finally, mix them all together. Serve immediately.

VARIATION

Alternative dressings for this salad can be made with 4 tbsp olive oil, 4 tbsp red wine, 4 tbsp red wine vinegar, and 1 tbsp sugar. Or, substitute 3 tbsp olive oil and 1 tbsp walnut or hazelnut oil for the olive oil.

Dolcelatte, Nut & Pasta Salad

Serves 4

INGREDIENTS

2 cups dried pasta shells
1 tbsp olive oil
1 cup shelled and halved
    walnuts

mixed salad greens, such
    as radicchio, escarole,
    arugula, corn salad, and
    frisée
8 ounces dolcelatte cheese,
    crumbled
salt

DRESSING:
2 tbsp walnut oil
4 tbsp extra virgin olive oil
2 tbsp red wine vinegar
salt and pepper

1 Bring a large saucepan of lightly salted water to a boil. Add the pasta shells and olive oil and cook until just tender, but still firm to the bite. Drain the pasta, rinse under cold running water, drain again, and set aside.

2 Spread out the shelled walnut halves on a cookie sheet and toast under a preheated broiler for about 2–3 minutes. Set aside to cool slightly while you make the dressing.

3 To make the dressing, whisk together the walnut oil, olive oil, and vinegar in a small bowl, and season with salt and pepper to taste.

4 Arrange the salad greens in a large serving bowl. Pile the cooled pasta in the middle of the salad greens and sprinkle the dolcelatte cheese on top. Pour the dressing over the pasta salad, scatter with the walnut halves and toss

together well to mix. Serve immediately.

COOK'S TIP

Dolcelatte is a semisoft, blue-veined cheese from Italy. Its texture is creamy and smooth and the flavor is delicate, but piquant. You could substitute Roquefort as an alternative. Whichever cheese you choose, it is essential that it is of the best quality and in peak condition.

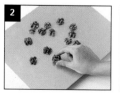

Goat Cheese with Penne, Pear, & Walnut Salad

Serves 4

INGREDIENTS

9 ounces dried penne	2 ripe pears, cored and diced	1 small onion, sliced
5 tbsp olive oil	1 fresh basil sprig	1 large carrot, grated
1 head radicchio, torn into pieces	1 bunch of watercress, trimmed	9 ounces goat cheese, diced
1 Webbs lettuce, torn into pieces	2 tbsp lemon juice	salt and pepper
7 tbsp chopped walnuts	3 tbsp garlic vinegar	
	4 tomatoes, quartered	

1 Bring a large saucepan of lightly salted water to a boil. Add the penne and 1 tbsp of the olive oil and cook until tender, but still firm to the bite. Drain the pasta, rinse under cold running water, drain thoroughly again, and set aside to cool.

2 Place the radicchio and Webbs lettuce in a large salad bowl and mix together well. Top with the pasta, walnuts, pears, basil, and watercress.

3 Mix together the lemon juice, the remaining olive oil, and the vinegar in a pitcher. Pour the mixture over the salad ingredients and toss thoroughly to coat the salad greens well.

4 Add the tomato quarters, onion slices, grated carrot, and diced goat cheese and toss together, using 2 forks, until well mixed. Leave the salad to chill in the refrigerator for about 1 hour before serving.

Pasta & Garlic Mayo Salad

Serves 4

INGREDIENTS

2 large lettuce heads	juice of 4 lemons	$1^1/8$ cups fresh garlic
9 ounces dried penne	1 head of celery, sliced	mayonnaise (see Cook's
1 tbsp olive oil	$3/4$ cup shelled, halved	Tip, below right)
8 red delicious apples	walnuts	salt

1 Wash, drain, and pat dry the lettuce leaves with paper towels. Transfer them to the refrigerator for 1 hour until crisp.

2 Meanwhile, bring a large saucepan of lightly salted water to a boil. Add the pasta and olive oil and cook until tender, but still firm to the bite. Drain the pasta and rinse under cold running water. Drain thoroughly again and set aside.

3 Core and dice the apples, place them in a small bowl, and sprinkle with the lemon juice. Mix together the pasta, celery, apples, and walnuts and toss the mixture in the garlic mayonnaise (see Cook's Tip, right). Add more mayonnaise, if desired.

4 Line a salad bowl with the lettuce leaves and spoon the pasta salad into the lined bowl. Serve.

COOK'S TIP

Sprinkling the apples with lemon juice will prevent them from turning brown.

COOK'S TIP

To make homemade garlic mayonnaise, beat 2 egg yolks with a pinch of salt and 6 crushed garlic cloves. Start beating in $1^1/2$ cups olive oil, 1–2 tsp at a time, using a balloon whisk or electric mixer. When about one-quarter of the oil has been fully incorporated, beat in 1–2 tbsp white wine vinegar. Continue beating in the oil, adding it in a thin, continuous stream. Finally, stir in 1 tsp Dijon mustard and season to taste with salt and pepper.

Fusilli, Avocado, Tomato, & Mozzarella Salad

Serves 4

INGREDIENTS

2 tbsp pine nuts
1 1/2 cups dried fusilli
1 tbsp olive oil
6 tomatoes
8 ounces mozzarella cheese
1 large avocado

2 tbsp lemon juice
3 tbsp chopped fresh basil
salt and pepper
fresh basil sprigs, to garnish

DRESSING:
6 tbsp extra virgin olive oil
2 tbsp white wine vinegar
1 tsp wholegrain mustard
pinch of sugar

1 Spread the pine nuts out on a cookie sheet and toast under a preheated broiler for 1–2 minutes. Remove and set aside to cool.

2 Bring a large saucepan of lightly salted water to a boil. Add the fusilli and olive oil and cook until tender, but still firm to the bite. Drain the pasta and rinse in cold water. Drain the pasta again and then set aside to cool slightly.

3 Thinly slice the tomatoes and the mozzarella cheese.

4 Cut the avocado in half, remove the pit, and skin. Cut into thin slices lengthwise and sprinkle with lemon juice to prevent discoloration.

5 To make the dressing, whisk together the oil, vinegar, mustard, and sugar in a small bowl, and season to taste.

6 Arrange the tomatoes, mozzarella cheese, and avocado alternately in overlapping slices on a large serving platter.

7 Toss the pasta with half of the dressing and the chopped basil, and season to taste. Spoon the pasta into the center of the platter and pour the remaining dressing on top. Sprinkle with the pine nuts, garnish with fresh basil sprigs, and serve.

Pasta-stuffed Tomatoes

Serves 4

INGREDIENTS

5 tbsp extra virgin olive oil,
plus extra for greasing
8 beef tomatoes or large
round tomatoes
1 cup dried ditalini or other
very small pasta shapes

8 black olives, pitted and finely
chopped
2 tbsp finely chopped fresh
basil
1 tbsp finely chopped fresh
parsley

²/3 cup freshly grated
Parmesan cheese
salt and pepper
fresh basil sprigs, to garnish

1 Brush a cookie sheet with olive oil.

2 Slice the tops off the tomatoes and reserve to make "lids." If the tomatoes will not stand up, cut a thin slice off the bottom of each tomato.

3 Scoop out the tomato pulp into a strainer, but do not pierce the tomato shells. Invert the tomato shells onto paper towels, pat dry, and then set aside to drain thoroughly.

4 Bring a large saucepan of lightly salted water to a boil. Add the ditalini or other pasta and 1 tbsp of the remaining olive oil and cook until tender, but still firm to the bite. Drain the pasta and set aside.

5 Put the olives, basil, parsley, and Parmesan cheese into a mixing bowl and stir in the drained tomato pulp. Add the pasta to the bowl. Stir in remaining olive oil, mix well, and season to taste.

6 Spoon the pasta mixture into the tomato shells and replace the lids. Arrange the tomatoes on the cookie sheet and bake in a preheated oven at 375°F for 15–20 minutes.

7 Remove the tomatoes from the oven and allow to cool until just warm. Arrange on a serving dish, garnish with the basil sprigs, and serve.

Rare Beef Pasta Salad

Serves 4

INGREDIENTS

1 pound rump or sirloin steak
in one piece
1 pound dried fusilli
5 tbsp olive oil
2 tbsp lime juice

2 tbsp Thai fish sauce (see
Cook's Tip)
2 tsp clear honey
4 scallions, sliced
1 cucumber, peeled and cut
into 1-inch chunks

3 tomatoes, cut into wedges
3 tsp finely chopped fresh
mint
salt and pepper

1 Season the steak with salt and black pepper. Broil or pan-fry the steak for 4 minutes on each side. Set aside for 5 minutes, then slice thinly across the grain.

2 Bring a large saucepan of lightly salted water to a boil. Add the fusilli and 1 tbsp of the olive oil and cook until tender, but still firm to the bite. Drain the fusilli, rinse in cold water, and drain again thoroughly. Toss the fusilli in the remaining olive oil.

3 Combine the lime juice, fish sauce, and honey in a small saucepan and cook over a medium heat for 2 minutes.

4 Add the scallions, cucumber, tomatoes, and mint to the pan, then add the sliced steak and mix thoroughly. Season to taste with salt.

5 Transfer the fusilli to a large, warm serving dish and top with the steak and salad mixture. Serve warm or allow to cool.

COOK'S TIP

Thai fish sauce, also known as nam pla, *is made from salted anchovies and has quite a strong flavor, so it should be used with discretion. It is available from some supermarkets and from Oriental food stores.*

Beet Cannolicchi

Serves 4

INGREDIENTS

11 ounces dried ditalini rigati
5 tbsp olive oil
2 garlic cloves, chopped
14 ounce can chopped
   tomatoes
14 ounces cooked beet, diced

2 tbsp chopped fresh basil
   leaves
1 tsp mustard seeds
salt and pepper

TO SERVE:
mixed salad greens, tossed in
   olive oil
4 Italian plum tomatoes, sliced

1 Bring a large pan of lightly salted water to a boil. Add the pasta and 1 tbsp of the oil and cook for about 10 minutes, until tender, but still firm to the bite. Drain and set aside.

2 Heat the remaining olive oil in a large saucepan. Add the garlic and sauté for 3 minutes. Add the chopped tomatoes and cook for 10 minutes.

3 Remove the pan from the heat and add the beet, basil, mustard seeds,

and pasta, and salt and black pepper.

4 Serve on a bed of mixed salad greens tossed in olive oil, and sliced plum tomatoes.

COOK'S TIP

Mustard seeds come from three different plants and may be black, brown, or white. Black and brown mustard seeds have a stronger, more pungent flavor than white mustard.

COOK'S TIP

To cook raw beet, trim off the leaves about 2 inches above the root and ensure that the skin is not broken. Boil in very lightly salted water for 30–40 minutes, until tender. Leave to cool and rub off the skin.

Desserts

If desserts do not usually spring to your mind when you think about cooking with pasta, you will be amazed by the wonderfully self-indulgent sweet treats in this chapter. Who could resist Honey & Walnut Nests, a scrumptious combination of pistachio nuts, honey, and crisp angel hair pasta? Raspberry Fusilli is a feast for the eyes as well as the taste buds, German Noodle Pudding is a rich and satisfying dessert based on a traditional Jewish recipe, and Baked Sweet Ravioli is a revelation to anyone with a sweet tooth. The recipes in this chapter will convince you that pasta desserts are much more exciting than a macaroni milk pudding, and your family and guests will be delighted with such imaginative ways to end a meal.

Baked Sweet Ravioli

Serves 4

INGREDIENTS

PASTA:
3³/4 cups all-purpose flour
10 tbsp butter, plus extra for
  greasing
³/4 cup superfine sugar
4 eggs

1 ounce yeast
¹/2 cup warm milk

FILLING:
²/3 cup chestnut purée
¹/2 cup cocoa powder
¹/4 cup superfine sugar

¹/2 cup chopped almonds
1 cup crushed amaretti
  cookies
⁵/8 cup orange marmalade

1 To make the sweet pasta dough, sift the flour into a mixing bowl, then mix in the butter, sugar, and 3 eggs.

2 Mix together the yeast and warm milk in a small bowl, then, mix into the dough.

3 Knead the dough for 20 minutes, cover with a clean cloth, and set aside in a warm place for 1 hour to rise.

4 Mix together the chestnut purée, cocoa powder, sugar, almonds, crushed amaretti cookies, and orange marmalade in a separate bowl.

5 Lightly grease a cookie sheet with butter.

6 Lightly flour the counter. Roll out the pasta dough into a thin sheet and then cut into 2-inch rounds with a plain pastry cutter.

7 Put a spoonful of filling onto each round and then fold in half, pressing the edges to seal. Arrange on the prepared cookie sheet, spacing the ravioli out well.

8 Beat the remaining egg and brush all over the ravioli to glaze. Bake in a preheated oven at 350°F for 20 minutes. Serve hot.

German Noodle Pudding

Serves 4

INGREDIENTS

4 tbsp butter, plus extra
    for greasing
6 ounces ribbon egg noodles
$^1/_2$ cup cream cheese
1 cup cottage cheese
$^1/_2$ cup superfine sugar
2 eggs, lightly beaten

$^1/_2$ cup sour cream
1 tsp vanilla extract
a pinch of ground cinnamon
1 tsp grated lemon rind
$^1/_4$ cup slivered almonds

$^3/_8$ cup dry white
    breadcrumbs
confectioner's sugar, for
    dusting

1 Grease an ovenproof dish with butter.

2 Bring a large pan of water to a boil. Add the noodles and cook until almost tender. Drain and set aside.

3 Beat together the cream cheese, cottage cheese, and sugar in a mixing bowl. Beat in the eggs, a little at a time. Stir in the sour cream, vanilla extract, cinnamon, and lemon rind, and fold in the noodles. Transfer the mixture to the prepared dish and smooth the surface.

4 Melt the butter in a skillet. Add the almonds and fry, stirring constantly, for about 1–1½ minutes, until lightly colored. Remove the skillet from the heat and stir the breadcrumbs into the almonds.

5 Sprinkle the almond and breadcrumb mixture over the pudding and bake in a preheated oven at 350°F for about 35–40 minutes, until just set. Dust with a little confectioner's sugar and serve immediately.

VARIATION

Although not authentic, you could add 3 tbsp raisins with the lemon rind in step 3, if desired.

Honey & Walnut Nests

Serves 4

INGREDIENTS

8 ounces angel hair pasta	1/2 cup sugar	salt
8 tbsp butter	1/3 cup clear honey	strained, plain yogurt, to serve
1 1/2 cups shelled pistachio nuts, chopped	5/8 cup water	
	2 tsp lemon juice	

1 Bring a large pan of lightly salted water to a boil. Add the angel hair pasta and cook until tender, but still firm to the bite. Drain and return to the pan. Add the butter and toss to coat the pasta. Set aside to cool.

2 Arrange 4 small flan or poaching rings on a cookie sheet. Divide the angel hair pasta into 8 equal quantities and spoon 4 of them into the rings. Press down lightly. Top the pasta with half of the nuts, then add the remaining pasta.

3 Bake in a preheated oven at 350°F for 45 minutes, until golden brown.

4 Meanwhile, put the sugar, honey, and water in a saucepan and bring to a boil over a low heat, stirring constantly until the sugar has dissolved completely. Simmer for 10 minutes, add the lemon juice, and simmer for a further 5 minutes.

5 Carefully transfer the angel hair nests to a serving dish. Pour the honey syrup on top, sprinkle with the remaining nuts, and set aside to cool completely before serving. Serve the strained, plain yogurt separately.

COOK'S TIP

Angel hair pasta is also known as capelli d'angelo. *Long and very fine, it is usually sold in small bunches that already resemble nests.*

Raspberry Fusilli

Serves 4

INGREDIENTS

1/2 cup dried fusilli	1 tbsp lemon juice	3 tbsp raspberry liqueur
4 cups raspberries	4 tbsp slivered almonds	salt
2 tbsp superfine sugar		

1 Bring a large pan of lightly salted water to a boil. Add the fusilli and cook until tender, but still firm to the bite. Drain the fusilli thoroughly, return to the pan, and set aside to cool.

2 Using a spoon, firmly press 1⅓ cups of the raspberries through a strainer set over a large mixing bowl to form a smooth purée.

3 Put the raspberry purée and sugar in a small saucepan and simmer over a low heat, stirring occasionally, for 5 minutes.

Stir in the lemon juice and set the sauce aside until required.

4 Add the remaining raspberries to the fusilli in the pan and mix together well. Transfer the raspberry and fusilli mixture to a serving dish.

5 Spread the almonds out on a cookie sheet and toast under the broiler until golden brown. Remove and set aside to cool slightly.

6 Stir the raspberry liqueur into the reserved raspberry sauce

and mix together until smooth. Pour the raspberry sauce over the fusilli, sprinkle the toasted almonds on top and serve.

VARIATION

You could use almost any sweet, really ripe berry for making this dessert. Strawberries and blackberries are especially suitable, combined with the correspondingly flavored liqueur. Alternatively, you could use a different berry with the fusilli, but still pour raspberry sauce on top.

Index

Index compiled by Hilary Bird.